Collins
LITTLE BOOKS

C000128189

English
History

HarperCollins Publishers
Westerhill Road
Bishopbriggs
Glasgow
G64 2QT

HarperCollins Publishers
Macken House, 39/40 Mayor Street Upper
Dublin 1, D01 C9W8, Ireland

First Edition 2018

10 9 8

© HarperCollins Publishers 2018

ISBN 978-0-00-829813-5

Collins® is a registered trademark of
HarperCollins Publishers Limited

www.collins.co.uk

A catalogue record for this book is
available from the British Library

Author: Robert Peal

Typeset by Davidson Publishing
Solutions

Printed and bound in India

MIX
Paper | Supporting
responsible forestry
FSC™ C007454

This book is produced from independently certified FSC™ paper
to ensure responsible forest management.

For more information visit: www.harpercollins.co.uk/green

Contents

Introduction

'This royal throne of kings, this scepter'd isle... This precious stone set in the silver sea... This blessed plot, this earth, this realm, this England'
William Shakespeare, *Richard II*

In his paean to England in Shakespeare's *Richard II*, John of Gaunt emphasises the importance of England's status as an 'island nation'. He is right to do so. So much of England's history has been dictated by its position on a small, rainy island off the western coast of Europe.

England's early history saw its shores invaded by waves of foreign settlers. The Romans arrived with Julius Caesar, followed by the Anglo-Saxons, the Vikings, and finally the Normans in 1066. This has given England an unusual mixture of Latin, French and Germanic influences. Days of the week in English are named after Norse Gods, but the months have Roman origins. The structure of the English language comes from Germany, but much of its vocabulary from France.

England's status as an island nation has offered it unrivalled defences against foreign invaders, such as Phillip II of Spain in 1588, Napoleon Bonaparte in 1805,

and Adolf Hitler in 1940. Unless you count the peaceful invasion of William and Mary in 1688, England has not been successfully invaded for one thousand years. The natural protection of the seas has given English history a stability and continuity that is unusual amongst the nations of Europe. The English Parliament has been meeting in Westminster since the 13th century, and the last battle fought on British soil was the defeat of Bonnie Prince Charlie at the Battle of Culloden in 1746.

England always depended upon its navy more than its army for protection, and for this reason the English people have long celebrated sailors as national heroes, such as Sir Francis Drake, Sir Walter Raleigh, Captain Cook and Lord Nelson. Britain's seafaring tradition came into its own when the countries of Europe began building global empires. From the mid-18th century onwards, the Royal Navy lay behind Britain's emergence as a world superpower, building an Empire stretching across North America, Africa, Asia and Australia. Today, Britain's multi-racial society with large Caribbean, Pakistani, Bangladeshi, Chinese and Indian populations is a direct legacy of its time as a sea-faring Empire.

Any book on the history of England will encounter difficulty negotiating England's appearance, and then disappearance, as a single political unit. England only emerged as one country, governed by one ruler, during the reign of Alfred the Great's grandson, King Athelstan. If you were to pinpoint England's birthdate, then King Athelstan's victory against the Vikings at the Battle of Brunanburh in AD 937 is perhaps the best contender. For this reason, this book gives relatively brief treatment to the history of 'England' prior to 937, offering a brief outline of the prehistoric, Roman, and early Anglo-Saxon periods in order to set the scene for England's emergence during the 10th century.

England's status as a sovereign state ended in 1707, when the Act of Union fused England and Wales with Scotland to form a new nation: Great Britain. From this point onwards in the book, I cease to write so often of 'England', as so many actions – in particular the creation of a global Empire – were really carried out by Britain. However, even though England ceased to be a sovereign state in 1707, it remains a country, with distinct traditions, culture, and – perhaps most importantly! – international sports.

ENGLISH HISTORY

10,000 BC | Prehistoric England

Around 12,000 years ago, the last Ice Age ended, and the British Isles once again became inhabited by humans. No written records of life in England exist from before the Roman invasion in 55 BC, so prehistoric England is a mysterious and unknowable place. But prehistoric Britons did leave their mark in other ways. Some lived in earthwork defensive settlements such as Maiden Castle in Dorset, some left behind enormous burial mounds for the dead. Prehistoric Britons were also skilled metalworkers, creating beautiful jewellery out of twisted gold thread. Tribal leaders would wear a thick golden ring called a 'torc' around their neck. There are also the remains of up to 900 stone circles built by prehistoric Britons, thought to have been used for religious and ceremonial purposes.

The warrior culture in prehistoric Britain can be seen from the swords, spears, shields and helmets uncovered by archaeologists. We also know that warriors rode horses and used chariots for battle. Two of the greatest artefacts uncovered dating from this period were found in the River Thames in London: a ceremonial bronze horned helmet found beside Waterloo Bridge, and a beautiful ceremonial shield decorated with coloured red glass, which was found in the Thames at Battersea.

3,000 BC | Stonehenge

The most famous monument from prehistoric England is Stonehenge in Wiltshire. The first stage of its construction began in 3,000 BC, and it originally consisted of eighty-two stones arranged in two rings. Extraordinarily, these stones – which weighed up to four tonnes each – are thought to have been dragged to Wiltshire all the way from South Wales. Most of Stonehenge as we see it today was constructed from stones brought from 19 miles away in the Marlborough Downs. The heaviest stone weighs fifty tonnes, and would have required 500 people to drag it on rollers and sledges to Stonehenge.

Inside Stonehenge, archaeologists have uncovered pits containing pieces of flint and red clay, probably used as religious offerings. Some of these pits contained the cremated remains of people. In addition, there are numerous Bronze Age burial mounds nearby, often placed on high ground overlooking the monument. Stonehenge was clearly a site of great religious and ceremonial importance, perhaps used for funeral ceremonies. Some archaeologists believe Stonehenge was used to observe the movements of the sun and the moon, with special ceremonies held at the monument on the Summer and Winter solstices (the longest and shortest days of the year).

By the 1st century BC, Roman civilisation was reaching its zenith, and the Roman Empire spread across Western Europe to the Middle East and North Africa. Meanwhile, Britain remained a prehistoric civilisation, inhabited by a people sometimes referred to today as 'Celts'. The first Roman to lead an expedition to Britain was the Governor of Gaul, Julius Caesar. In 54 BC, Caesar invaded Britain with an army of around 37,000 troops and won the surrender of its Southern tribes. However, Caesar had to return to Italy, and his conquest of Britain was left incomplete.

A century later in AD 43, the Roman Emperor Claudius set his sights on conquering Britain, in part to gain possession of its wealthy gold, silver and tin mines. An invasion force of 40,000 Roman soldiers landed in Britain, which Emperor Claudius later joined with a force of elephants – intended to scare the Britons into submission! For the next four centuries, Roman power spread across England and Wales, all the way to Hadrian's Wall near today's border with Scotland. Some remains of Roman rule can be seen today in locations such as Fishbourne Palace in West Sussex, Porchester Castle in Hampshire, and the beautiful Roman baths in Bath.

AD 61 | Boudicca

It was only during the 16th century that the story of Boudicca, the famous warrior queen, was uncovered in the writings of the Roman historian Tacitus. Boudicca was the Queen of the Iceni tribe in modern-day Norfolk. The invading Romans were unwilling to respect the authority of a female leader, so they confiscated Boudicca's land, publically beat her, and – worst of all – raped her two daughters. Boudicca was outraged, and her Iceni tribe rose up in rebellion, destroying the nearby Roman capital of Camulodonum (Colchester). Boudicca and her rebel army then burnt to the ground the Roman trading settlement of Londinium (London), before turning northwards, and destroying the Roman settlement of Verulamium (St Albans).

According to Roman historians, Boudicca was tall and fierce, with a mass of tawny hair flowing down to her hips. Tribes flocked from across southern Britain to join their defiant warrior queen. Boudicca's final showdown with the Roman army took place somewhere in the Midlands, but the well-drilled Roman army was too much for the Britons. They were massacred, and Boudicca and her daughters poisoned themselves rather than falling into the hands of the Roman soldiers. With Boudicca's rebellion defeated, the Roman conquest could now continue.

410 | Legend of King Arthur

By the 5th century, Rome was under attack from the barbarian tribes of northern Europe. In 410, the Roman Emperor ordered Roman legions stationed in Britain to abandon the country and return to Rome to help in the city's defence. A small population of Romano-British citizens were left in Britain, but they were unable to defend themselves from a new invasion force from Northern Germany attacking Britain's shores – the Anglo-Saxons.

It was from this tumultuous period of history that England's most potent legend emerged: the tale of King Arthur. If he existed at all, King Arthur may have been a Romano-British military ruler who led the defence of Britain against invading Anglo-Saxons during the 5th century. However, over the centuries medieval poets, artists and storytellers added layers of myth and legend to this outline, keen to reshape Arthur in their own image. Arthur's story was embellished by the wizard Merlin, Arthur's wife Guinevere, the gallant knight Sir Lancelot, and the legend of the Sword in the Stone – none of which has any grounding in historical records. Even Arthur's Round Table, which can be visited in Winchester Castle, was created around 1290 during the reign of Edward I.

After the Roman army abandoned Britain in 410, two tribes from Northern Germany began to invade and settle in England. Known as the Anglo-Saxons, they established a number of separate kingdoms across the country, such as Wessex in the south, Mercia in the midlands, and Northumbria in the Northeast. Early Anglo-Saxon England had a population of perhaps one million people living scattered across the countryside, in houses made of wood and straw.

Unlike the Romans, the early Anglo-Saxons could not read or write, and did not have the technology to build cities or roads. There are no written records or buildings left from this period for historians to study, so some call the early Anglo-Saxon period the 'Dark Ages'. Much of what we know about early Anglo-Saxon England comes from the findings of archaeologists. Anglo-Saxons were skilled metal workers who loved jewellery and made beautiful objects out of gold and gems. Perhaps the most famous Anglo-Saxon artefact is an iron helmet and patterned facemask found in 1939 at a burial mound in Suffolk called Sutton Hoo. The Sutton Hoo helmet was intricately decorated with scenes of war, such as a warrior on a horse trampling a fallen enemy.

597 | The arrival of Christianity

At first, the Anglo-Saxons were pagans, who believed in the Norse gods. Woden was the King of the Gods, but there was also Tiw the god of war, Freya the goddess of love and fertility, and Thor the god of thunder. The days of the week in English are still named after these gods: Tiw became Tuesday, Woden became Wednesday, Thor became Thursday, and Freya became Friday.

This began to change when Pope Gregory in Rome sent a monk named Augustine to convert the Anglo-Saxons to Christianity. Augustine landed on the south coast of England in 597 with a group of around forty monks. Here, Augustine met Ethelbert, the King of Kent. Ethelbert's wife, a princess from France called Bertha, was already a Christian. Under Bertha and Augustine's influence, Ethelbert became the first Anglo-Saxon king to convert to Christianity. In 635, a monk called Aidan brought Christianity to Northumbria from Ireland. Pope Gregory made Augustine the first Archbishop of Canterbury, and Kent and Northumbria became the centres of Christianity in England, from which this new religion eventually spread throughout the whole country. To this day, the Archbishop of Canterbury remains the leader of the Church of England.

793 | Viking raids

In January 793, a band of warriors attacked the Christian monastery on the Holy Island of Lindisfarne in Northumbria. They arrived from the sea in ships with dragon heads carved into the bows, heavily armed with metal helmets, armour and two-handed axes. The warriors broke into the monastery, drowning the older monks in the sea and taking the younger monks as slaves. They then stole Lindisfarne's treasures, and sailed away.

For the next three centuries, Anglo-Saxon England was subject to repeated waves of attacks from these warriors. Known as Vikings, they sailed to Britain from Scandinavia in longboats – huge ships that used both oars and sails to travel great distances along rivers and across the seas. At first, Vikings were content with hit-and-run raids on English coastal towns and monasteries. However, in 865, the Vikings assembled a force to settle in England, known as the 'Great Heathen Army'. The Great Heathen Army captured the city of York in 867, and used it as a base to spread their power throughout northern England. Known as 'Jorvik' to the Vikings, York became a thriving centre of overseas trade under Viking rule, and home to perhaps 15,000 people.

899 | Alfred the Great

Alfred became King of Wessex, an Anglo-Saxon kingdom in the south of England, in 871. Aged only 23, he was immediately thrown into the long-running war with the Viking Great Heathen Army, who had by now settled throughout much of England. In 878, a Viking army led by King Guthram attacked King Alfred in Chippenham while he was celebrating Twelfth Night, the last day of Christmas. Alfred escaped the attack, but many of his men were slaughtered. Almost defeated, Alfred retreated to the marshes of Somerset, where he began to organise his counter-attack. Later that year, Alfred defeated Guthram's Vikings at the Battle of Edington.

Alfred and Guthrum agreed to divide England by a diagonal line from the mouth of the River Mersey in the north-west, to the mouth of the Thames in the south-east. Alfred ruled the land to the south of this line, and fortified it against any future Viking attacks. In 899, Alfred died. His defeat of the Vikings, and rule of Wessex laid the foundation on which his descendants would build the unified Anglo-Saxon Kingdom of England. Today, Alfred remains the only king in English history to be remembered as 'the Great'.

Following King Alfred's death in 899, it fell to his son King Edward the Elder to continue the fight against the Vikings. Edward was greatly helped by his older sister Æthelflæd, who ruled much of the English Midlands as the 'Lady of Mercia'. Famed for her intelligence and strength, Æthelflæd led her armies into battle against the Vikings, winning back their land for the Anglo-Saxons. King Edward was so impressed by his tough older sister Æthelflaed that he sent his own son, Athelstan, to be brought up by her.

Though he is not much talked about today, some historians say Athelstan should be remembered as the first King of England. When Athelstan became king, Northumbria remained an outpost of Viking power centred around the Viking capital of Jorvik. Athelstan gradually asserted Anglo-Saxon power over Northumbria, and in 937 he won a great victory at the Battle of Brunanburh, against an enormous Scottish, Viking and Northumbrian army. During his reign, Athelstan had new coins minted for his kingdom, on which he gave himself the title Rex Anglorum, meaning 'King of the English'. For the first time since the Roman conquest, England could be described as a unified country under the rule of a single leader.

1042 | Edward the Confessor

In 1042, the English throne returned to Anglo-Saxon rule under Edward the Confessor. Edward the Confessor was mild-mannered, middle-aged, and extremely religious – hence his title 'Confessor'. This intense religious faith may explain why King Edward remained childless even after he married. Edward's failure to provide an heir set the scene for perhaps the most famous event in English history.

As Edward the Confessor drifted into old age, three claimants started jockeying for the right to succeed him as King of England. Firstly, there was Harold Godwinson, the Earl of Wessex. Harold was a powerful Anglo-Saxon nobleman, and brother-in-law to the king through his sister Edith. Second, there was William Duke of Normandy, a ruthless warrior from France who claimed to have been promised the throne by King Edward back in 1051. Lastly, there was the King of Norway Harald Hardrada, who wanted to return England to Viking rule.

Edward the Confessor did leave England another historic legacy, aside from an uncertain throne. His life's work was the construction of Westminster Abbey, consecrated in December 1065, one week before Edward's death. When completed, Westminster Abbey was the largest church in northern Europe, and has witnessed the coronation of every English monarch since 1066.

1066 | King Harold

Edward the Confessor died on 5th January 1066. As he lay dying, Edward bequeathed his throne to Harold Godwinson, the Earl of Wessex. On 6th January, Harold was crowned King at Westminster Abbey. He was to be England's last Anglo-Saxon king.

The Godwin family were known for their ruthless ambition, but lacked royal blood. Many feared that seizing the English throne had been a step too far. These fears appeared to be confirmed in April 1066 when a burning comet appeared in the night's sky. Was this a bad omen, showing God's anger that an illegitimate king now sat on the English throne?

In September 1066, a Viking invasion force led by Harold Hardrada sailed up the Humber River and took York. Hardrada was accompanied by Harold Godwinson's treacherous younger brother, Tostig. Harold marched his Anglo-Saxon army north to meet the Vikings, and caught them by surprise on the morning of 25th September at a location named Stamford Bridge. The Anglo-Saxons won a great victory, annihilating the Viking force and killing both Tostig and Hardrada. But this victorious start to Harold's reign did not last long.

1066 | Battle of Hastings

No sooner had King Harold vanquished the Viking invaders, he received news that the Duke of Normandy's invasion force had landed on the south-east coast of England. Harold demanded that his army march the length of England in little over two weeks, and on 14th October they met the Norman invasion force 10 miles inland from the town of Hastings. This battle would decide the course of English history.

Harold's army of 7–8000 men men were weak and outnumbered by William's superior army, which included heavily armoured knights on horseback and archers. In all, the Normans numbered perhaps 10,000 men. Despite this, the Anglo-Saxons started well, creating a defensive shield wall on top of the high ground of Senlac Hill. However, repeated waves of Norman attack slowly broke the Saxon formation.

What happened next is hotly disputed. According to one story, Harold Godwinson was shot through the eye by an arrow, and then dismembered by Norman knights. This is what appears to be shown in the famous Bayeux Tapestry, a magnificent 70 metre-long embroidered cloth that was created to celebrate the Norman invasion (see picture). After six hours of brutal fighting, William Duke of Normandy was victorious.

On Christmas Day 1066, the Duke of Normandy was crowned King William I of England at Westminster Abbey. In the years that followed, William was brutally effective at spreading Norman power throughout his new kingdom. The Normans would respond to any Anglo-Saxon rebellion by descending on their community, burning down their villages and slaughtering their inhabitants.

Perhaps the most infamous occurrence of Norman cruelty took place in 1069, when William's newly appointed Earl of Northumbria was murdered by Anglo-Saxon rebels. William was furious, and vowed to make an example of the Northern rebels. His army marched north, and burnt to the ground every village between York and Durham. Farm animals were slaughtered, crops were destroyed, and the fields were laced with salt so that no more food could be grown. Known as the 'Harrying of the North', this event led to the starvation of perhaps 100,000 people.

Other examples of Anglo-Saxon rebellions and resistance took place, but all in vain. Through sheer military superiority, William's occupying force of 20,000 men were able to subdue a population of two million. England's era of Anglo-Saxon rule was firmly at an end.

1086 | Domesday Book

Having conquered England, William set about creating a new ruling class of Norman noblemen. William seized the land from England's Anglo-Saxon noblemen, many of whom had died fighting at Hastings, and transferred its ownership to his loyal Norman knights. Norman noblemen were given titles as Earls and Barons, and in the centre of their land they built large, intimidating castles to confirm their power. A strict social hierarchy (sometimes called the feudal system) was created, with Norman noblemen at the top, and their Anglo-Saxon vassals below.

To keep a record of this enormous transfer in land ownership, William the Conqueror ordered the Domesday Book to be written. For two years, Norman commissioners travelled the length and breadth of England, recording what this new kingdom contained down to the last pig, plough and beehive. Completed in 1086, it details the contents of over 13,000 different towns and villages. It is one of England's most valuable historical documents, providing an extraordinary picture of life in the 11th century. For example, in 1085 Birmingham was a small village with just nine families and two ploughs. Today, it is England's second largest city.

ɂ Grantebrigge ſyra. Jn ſtaple
ou hundr̄. iurauerunt homi
nes. ſcilicet Nicholaus de Kenet.
⁊ hugo de heſelinges. Wills de
ypcham. Warinus de Saham.
⁊ ɂ.t. de fordham. Ormar de bel
ingehā. Alanus de Buruuelle.
Aurie de ſnellenuelle. Prcotus
uiccomes ⁊ omnes franci ⁊
ingli.

ɂ Hoc hundreto nicholaus
.net de will de warenne p̄
ii. ⁊ dimid. ſe defendit t.r. e. ⁊
in p.ii. ⁊ dimidia. x. car̄. ibi. ē. i
v. in dominio. ⁊ v. uillanis.
vi. uillan. ⁊ i. pbr̄s. ⁊ xii. ſeru.
molend. ē. ibi. Hich reddit. p̄r̄
duabȝ. ē. pecunia in dominio.
vm. animal̄ ocioſa. ⁊ ccc. ⁊
iii. xx. oues. x. porc. iiii. runcin.
aſtum ⁊ ad pecun. uille. Jn to
s ualentii, vii. lib. ⁊ qn̄ recepit
v. li. ɂt. r. e. xii. li. Hoc mane
ii tenuit hobiluſ regiſ regiſ
eduuardi. Et in hoc manerio
ur̄ qd ſochemann̄ Godric̄. ho
. potuit dare ſine licentia dn̄i

lvii. nummoſ p conſuetu... ⁊ p̄
aimti.

ɂ hoc hundr̄. Ormar de comite
Alano. Belmegeſhā. p. iii. h. ⁊
dimi. vi. c̄. ſe defendit t.r.e. ⁊ in
p.ii. h. ⁊ dimi. vi. c̄. i eſt tr̄a. due
car̄. in dominio. ⁊ iiii. uill. xr.
uill. ⁊ vi. bor. vi. ſer. ⁊ ii. molend.
unū molend. ii. ſol. red. ⁊ aliud
moturā: in dominio. Pratum
duabȝ. ē. paſtura ad pecun̄ uille.
ii. animal̄ ocioſa. lx. o. xx. porc.
ii. runc. Jn totis ualentiis ualet
lx. ſol. ⁊ qn̄ recepit. lx. ſol. t.r.e.
c. ſol. Hoc manū tenuit Ormar
homo ɂelme. t.r. eaduuardi. potuit
dare tr̄ uoluit. ɂ n hoc hundr̄
ganfriduſ de mandauilla. cypelhā
x. h. tempe. r. e. ⁊ hee hide n̄ defen
derunt ſe iii p. v. h. ɂt uiccomes ip̄
uiccomitatuſ fec̄ haſ, x. h. defende
p v. h. t. r. e. xvii. c̄. eſt i tr̄a. iii. in
dominio. xiiii. uill. xxii. uillani.
xii. bor. vi. ſeru. Pratum iiii. car̄.
Paſtura ad pecuniā uille. c.iiii. an.
xv. porc. ccc. oues. xv. mun. iii. runc.
⁊ unū molend. de una piſtina.
mille anguille ⁊ dimid. Jn totis
ualentiis xx. lib. ⁊ qn̄ recep. xvi. lib.

1170 | Murder of Thomas Becket

Henry II was an energetic king, who rebuilt the power of the English monarchy after nineteen years of bloody civil war. But he is chiefly remembered for English history's most famous murder. As king, Henry II wanted to gain more power over the English Church, so in 1161 he made his loyal friend Thomas Becket the Archbishop of Canterbury (leader of the English Church). However, on becoming archbishop, Becket transformed into a pious defender of Church independence.

Becket refused to take orders from Henry II, and their friendship transformed into bitter hatred. During a particularly foul dispute in 1170, Henry II allegedly screamed 'will nobody rid me of this turbulent priest!' Four knights interpreted Henry II's outburst as an order, and rode to Canterbury Cathedral. They killed the Archbishop with a blow to the head by a sword, and smeared his brains across the Cathedral floor.

Henry II insisted that the murder of Thomas Becket was a tragic mistake, and did penance by walking barefoot to Canterbury where he was whipped by the Cathedral monks. Becket meanwhile was celebrated as a martyr for defending Church freedom, and made a Saint. His shrine became one of the most popular pilgrimage sites in medieval Europe.

1204 | Eleanor of Aquitaine

Henry II's wife, Eleanor of Aquitaine, was a remarkable Queen. In 1137, aged only fifteen, she married the King of France, Louis VII. However, Louis could not tolerate Eleanor's independent mindedness, and they divorced in 1152. Eight weeks later, Eleanor shocked medieval Europe by marrying the heir to the English throne, the future Henry II. Henry II and Eleanor's marriage started well having seven children together, but they began to quarrel. In 1174, Eleanor was arrested for plotting against her husband, and thrown in prison for sixteen years. When Henry II died, Eleanor's favourite son Richard the Lionheart became King of England, and freed his mother from imprisonment.

Richard the Lionheart, whose statue stands outside the Houses of Parliament, is one of England's most famous kings. However, he spent as little as six months actually in England during his ten-year reign. For most of the time, he was fighting on crusade in the Holy Land. Whilst Richard was fighting foreign wars, it was his mother, Eleanor of Aquitaine, who ruled England. She died in 1204 at the astonishing age of 82, having become one of the most powerful and respected figures, male or female, in all of Europe.

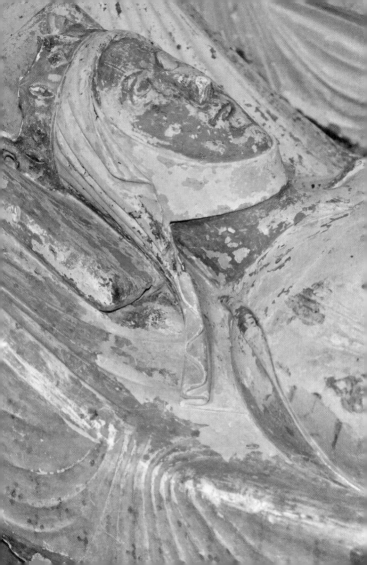

1215 | King John and the Magna Carta

No medieval King of England has as bad a reputation as King John. John was Henry II's youngest son, and became king in 1199 after the death of his older brother Richard the Lionheart. Many believed John's nephew Arthur had a better claim to the throne. Before long, rumours began to circulate that to secure his hold on power, John had drowned his own nephew in the River Seine.

John was ruthless in punishing those who opposed his rule, often starving his enemies to death in castle dungeons. He repeatedly argued with the Catholic Church, and was excommunicated by the Pope. Worst of all, John was a hopeless warrior, and lost much of England's territory in France, including his ancestral homeland in Normandy. To fight these unsuccessful wars, John taxed his Barons dry. But John's tyrannical rule did leave a positive legacy. In 1215, the Barons united against King John, and forced him to sign a series of promises known as the Magna Carta. These promises included the right to a fair trial, independence of the church, and the need to gain the Barons' consent before raising taxes. Today, the Magna Carta is seen as the birth of political rights in England.

The image opposite shows a memorial in Runnymede, the meadow beside the River Thames where King John agreed to the Magna Carta.

Did Robin Hood even exist? Probably not. However, the legend of Robin Hood was popular in England from the 15th century onwards, and tells us a lot about medieval attitudes towards tyrannical royal power. Robin Hood is the outlaw of Sherwood Forest, who steals from the rich to give to the poor. A skilled archer, Robin terrorises the Sheriff of Nottingham and his master, Prince John, who has taken the throne from his brother Richard the Lionheart. Robin Hood is helped by his band of 'merry men', including Little John (who is actually very tall), Much the Millar's son, and the rather less-than-pious Friar Tuck.

In later years, Robin Hood was depicted as a deposed Saxon nobleman, fighting back against oppressive Norman overlords. Woodlands such as Sherwood Forest were kept as royal hunting grounds by the royal kings, and those caught poaching on these grounds were cruelly punished. Today, you can visit the 'Major Oak', a hollow oak tree in Sherwood Forest where, according to legend, Robin and his merry men once hid. Sadly, Major Oak was not even an acorn during the reign of King John.

1265 | The first Parliament

King John's son Henry III was forced to reaffirm the Magna Carta (see page 38) in 1225, setting a precedent for all future English monarchs. Henry III had great military ambitions, wanting to reconquer the land lost by his father in France, go on a crusade to the Holy Land, and even make his son the king of Sicily. However, all of these foreign wars meant increases in taxation.

In 1264, a group of rebel barons led by the Earl of Leicester Simon de Montfort rose up against Henry III. At the Battle of Lewes, de Montfort defeated Henry III and took him prisoner. De Montfort then summoned all England's bishops and noblemen to London, along with representatives from every shire and borough in the land. On 20th January 1265 they met at Westminster Hall as a 'Parliament', taken from the French verb *parler* ('to speak').

De Montfort's Parliament is often called the first English Parliament. It gave institutional form to the promise in the Magna Carta that the monarch's government should seek the consent of its people before passing new laws and taxes. Parliament still represents this principle today.

1283 | The Conquest of Wales

Since 1066, the Norman monarchs repeatedly tried to conquer Wales, but with little success. By the 1260s, most of Wales was under the control of Llywelyn ap Gruffyd. As the Prince of Wales, Llywelyn was expected to pay homage to the English king, but when the young Edward I was crowned king of England in 1174, Llywelyn refused to do so. Edward I was a brutal and warlike king, and saw this provocation as an opportunity to bring England's troublesome neighbour under his control. In 1277, Edward invaded Wales with an enormous army. Five years later, Llywelyn was killed in battle, and his head was taken back to England to be displayed on a spike at the Tower of London. Llwyelyn's brother, Dafydd, carried on the fight until 1283, when Edward captured Davydd and had him hung, drawn and quartered.

Having conquered Wales, Edward set about building a series of enormous castles to secure his power. For this reason, Wales has the highest concentration of castles of any country in Europe. Edward did not get rid of the title 'Prince of Wales', but gave it to his eldest son, thus beginning the practice of giving this title to the heir to the English throne.

1337 | The Hundred Years War

Ever since the Duke of Normandy conquered England in 1066, English monarchs had held territories in France. This led to ongoing tension between the French and English Kings, which frequently spilled over into war. In 1328, King Charles IV of France died without a male heir, and his throne passed to the French Count of Valois, who became Philip VI of France. However, the English King Edward III, whose mother was a French princess, believed he had a stronger claim to the throne. In 1337, Edward III declared himself the rightful King of France, marking the start of the Hundred Years War.

Edward III was a charismatic military leader, and his armies won a series of victories throughout France. By 1360, almost one third of France was under English rule. Many of Edward III's victories could be put down to England's archers, whose 2 metre longbows could fire rapid waves of arrows at an advancing army, with a range of around 200 metres. Edward III was so dedicated to the longbow that he banned sports such as football from being played on Sundays, so that Englishmen of fighting age could practice their archery skills instead.

1348 | Order of the Garter

Tall, brave and handsome, Edward III was in many ways the quintessential medieval king. He also did more than any other king to create a glamorous culture of chivalry amongst his men, which was much inspired by the ever-popular medieval legend of King Arthur and his Knights of the Round Table. The medieval world of popular imagination, full of brave kings, virtuous knights, fair maidens and magnificent tournaments, was largely the creation of Edward III's reign.

On his return from a victorious campaign in France in 1348, Edward assembled his own military brotherhood of 25 knights, each chosen for their bravery on the battlefield. This brotherhood was named the 'Order of the Garter', and its first member was Edward's son, a celebrated warrior called the Black Prince.

Edward and his Order toured England, staging jousting tournaments in major towns. From Turkey, they took the legend of a Christian knight named George, who had slain a dragon, and made him their patron saint. Edward gave the Order its own chapel in Windsor, where each knight claimed a seat in the choir stalls, bedecked with their elaborate heraldic crests. St George's Chapel (image opposite) remains the site of many royal weddings and burials to this day.

1348 | The Black Death

In June 1348, inhabitants of the Dorset port town of Melcombe Regis began dying of a strange new disease. The first symptoms were large swellings known as 'buboes' said to resemble an onion, which appeared in victims' armpits and between their legs. These spread across the body, followed by blue or black blotches. Sufferers would start to vomit and spit blood, suffer from seizures, and their breath turned foul and stinking. After a few days of horrific suffering, they were dead.

The people of Melcombe Regis were England's first victims of the bubonic plague, or Black Death. This disease arrived in English ports from mainland Europe, transported by the fleas living on black rats, and rapidly spread inland. Nobody was safe from the Black Death. It claimed two Archbishops of Canterbury, and King Edward III's own daughter. Convinced that God was punishing them for their sins, the English people were thrown into panic and despair.

Whole communities were turned into ghost towns overnight. In some, it was said, there were not even enough survivors to bury the dead. Within two years, the Black Death had killed between one third and a half of England's population.

1381 | The Peasants' Revolt

In 1381, the fourteen-year-old King Richard II established a poll tax to pay for continued fighting in the Hundred Years War. The poll tax was a flat rate payment of 4p to be paid by all adults irrespective of income, which made it deeply unpopular amongst England's peasants.

In protest, thousands of peasants from Kent and Essex marched on London. Led by a Kentish yeoman named Wat Tyler, they rioted through London, storming Newgate and Westminster prisons, burning down the palace of the King's uncle John of Gaunt, and beheading the Archbishop of Canterbury and Lord High Treasurer, whose heads were placed on spikes and paraded through the city. Richard II agreed to meet with the rebels outside London at Smithfield. However, the negotiations turned into a struggle, during which Tyler was run through with a sword and killed. The image opposite shows Richard II with the rebels and the death of Wat Tyler.

Richard then promised the peasants that if they returned home, they would be pardoned of their crimes. The peasants duly did so, but Richard did not keep his word, and 200 of the revolt's leaders were tracked down and hanged. The Peasants' Revolt may have failed, but the social structure of feudal England had been dealt a historic blow.

1387 | *The Canterbury Tales*

Geoffrey Chaucer was the son of a London wine merchant, and he worked for the Royal Court as a civil servant and diplomat. Chaucer also wrote poetry for the entertainment of his Royal patrons, and began work on his masterpiece, *The Canterbury Tales*, in 1387. The extended poem follows a group of 30 pilgrims who gather at the Tabard Inn on the south side of London Bridge, before setting off on a pilgrimage to Canterbury to visit the shrine of Saint Thomas Becket (see page 34). Harry Bailey, the innkeeper, proposes a story-telling competition to keep them entertained during the pilgrimage. The best storyteller will be rewarded with a free supper at Bailey's inn on their return to London.

This structure allows Chaucer to produce a series of short stories, each painting a vivid portrait of medieval English society. There is the noble knight, the snobbish prioress, the much-married wife of Bath, and the vulgar miller tooting on his bagpipes. Chaucer's stories were written in vernacular English, not aristocratic French. Involving naked bottoms, trysts in pear trees, and corrupt religious figures, Chaucer's tales reveal a bawdy humour and cynicism that still feels remarkably 'English' six centuries later.

1415 | Agincourt

After the victories of Edward III in the Hundred Years War with France (see page 44), the English suffered a steady series of losses. This losing streak was briefly interrupted by the campaigns of Henry V. In August 1415, Henry V crossed the English Channel with 12,000 men, and took the French port of Harfleur. Things then turned against the English. Many of them were suffering from dysentery, so Henry embarked on a gruelling march north to the English-controlled port of Calais where they could spend the winter.

On 25th October, Henry's army , now nearer 7,000, was interrupted by an enormous French force of over 12,000 men. The English were tired, hungry and heavily outnumbered. Henry positioned his men behind a row of wooden palings, on a narrow strip of land fenced in by forests on either side. The French army were funnelled into a trap, and the English longbowmen rained arrows down on the enemy. Against the odds, the English won a startling victory.

Agincourt has since come into English memory due to Shakespeare's play *Henry V*, where Henry V gives his famous 'St Crispin's Day' speech. On the eve of battle, Shakespeare famously depicts Henry V addressing his men: 'We few, we happy few, we band of brothers.'

1459 | The Wars of the Roses

Henry V was succeeded by his son Henry VI. Unlike his heroic father, Henry VI hated the idea of war and refused to lead his army into battle. In 1453, the Hundred Years War ended with England's humiliating defeat, their French territories reduced to the small port town of Calais. To make matters worse, Henry VI suffered the first of many bouts of madness that year. He became completely unresponsive to anything around him, and had to be cared for like a new-born child.

This set in motion a crisis, during which the powerful nobleman Richard Duke of York began to organise opposition to the mad King Henry VI. Two rival factions emerged in the King's court. On one side were those loyal to the King and known as the House of Lancaster, later represented by a red rose. On the other side, those loyal to the House of York, later represented by a white rose. In 1459, the 'Wars of the Roses' began. Two years later, the House of York won a decisive victory at the brutal Battle of Towton – the single bloodiest battle ever fought on British soil. The Duke of York's son was crowned King Edward IV. The white rose was now in power.

1483 | The Princes in the Tower

Towards the end of the Wars of the Roses, one of the great mysteries in English history took place. On and off fighting between Lancaster and York continued throughout Edward IV's reign, but by the time he died in 1483, the House of York had a reasonable grip on the English throne. The throne should have passed to the King's twelve-year-old son, also called Edward. However, the young Prince Edward's uncle Richard Duke of Gloucester decided to take him and his younger brother into his care. The two princes were placed in the Tower of London 'for their own safety'. But then their uncle Richard declared his nephews illegitimate, and had himself crowned King Richard III.

In Shakespeare's play *Richard III*, the princes' uncle is depicted as a scheming villain: an ugly hunchback with a withered arm. To secure his place as King, Richard III orders that his nephews be smothered to death with their own pillows as they sleep. What really happened, we will probably never know. What we do know is that after the summer of 1483, the Princes were never seen again. Rumours quickly spread that Richard III had cruelly murdered his own nephews.

1485 | The Battle of Bosworth Field

During the reign of Richard III, an unlikely new claimant to the throne emerged from the House of Lancaster. Brought up in south Wales, Henry Tudor's claim to the throne was tenuous. However, he was a charismatic leader, and was greatly helped by his formidable mother Margaret Beaufort. Having planned his invasion from exile in France, Henry Tudor landed in Wales on 1st August, 1485. Three weeks later, he met King Richard III's Yorkist army at Bosworth Field, just outside Leicester. Henry's Lancastrian forces gained the upper hand, and Richard III was cornered, overpowered, and killed. His body was buried in a monastery on the outskirts of medieval Leicester, only to be rediscovered some 500 years later, in 2012, beneath a car park.

Henry Tudor was crowned King Henry VII of England on the battlefield at Bosworth. To bring an end to the thirty-year feud between the Houses of York and Lancaster, Henry married Elizabeth of York, who was the daughter of Edward IV. To symbolise this union between the two houses, Henry created the Tudor Rose: the white rose of York sitting within the red rose of Lancaster. The Tudors would now rule England for the next hundred years.

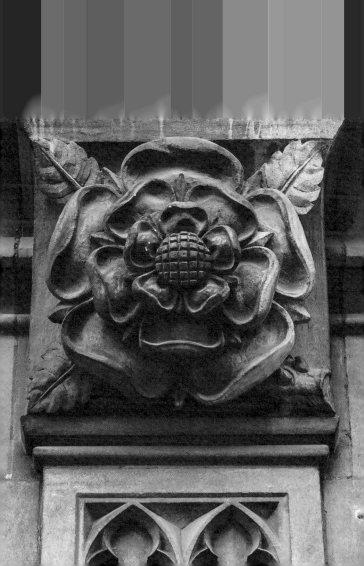

The Henry VIII who came to the English throne in 1509 was very different to the overweight, wife-killing tyrant of popular imagination. He was a handsome and athletic young prince who enjoyed sport, hunting and jousting. He was also intelligent and cultured, speaking many languages, writing poetry, and composing music. Henry VIII's major ambition as king was to reassert England's claim to rule France. Having allied with Spain and the Holy Roman Empire, Henry invaded France in 1513, winning a minor victory at the Battle of the Spurs. During this campaign, King James IV of Scotland took the opportunity to invade England. His army was soundly beaten at the Battle of Flodden by an English army under the command of Henry VIII's wife, Catherine.

Henry's ambition to rule France was derailed in 1516 when the shrewd and warlike Frances I became King of France. Henry VIII was persuaded to make peace with France. In 1520, Henry VIII met his great rival Francis I at a magnificent celebration of Anglo-French peace known as the Field of the Cloth of Gold (see image opposite), a two-week carnival of drinking, feasting and tournaments.

1534 | Anne Boleyn

Henry VIII's first wife Catherine of Aragon was seven years his senior, and by the late 1520s it was clear that she was not going to provide him with a male heir. Around this time, Henry VIII fell for one of Catherine's ladies in waiting, the intelligent and flirtatious Anne Boleyn (see image opposite). Henry VIII desperately desired to marry Anne, but first he would have to annul his marriage with Catherine. However, the Pope in Rome refused to grant Henry VIII his annulment.

Henry VIII was furious about his inability to marry Anne Boleyn. After years of struggling to convince the Pope to change his mind, Henry VIII finally decided to break away from the Catholic Church in 1534 so that he was no longer under the authority of Rome. This momentous event began the English Reformation (see page 64). The break with Rome allowed Henry VIII to marry Anne Boleyn. However, his affections for her soon waned. She provided him with a child, but it was a daughter (the future Elizabeth I), not the son Henry VIII so desperately desired. After two years of marriage, Anne Boleyn was beheaded in 1536 on trumped up charges of adultery.

1534 | The English Reformation

Henry VIII's decision to leave the Roman Catholic Church in 1534 triggered the greatest religious upheaval in English history. England was set on a new path towards Protestantism, which rejected the rituals, doctrines, images and superstitions of the Catholic Church. In a burst of religious destruction, over 900 monasteries were destroyed, with their nuns and monks turned onto the streets. Church treasures were melted down, statues were smashed, Latin prayer books were burnt, and medieval wall paintings were covered with whitewash. This process intensified during the reign of Henry VIII's son, Edward VI.

Through seizing land that had once belonged to the monasteries, and selling on their possessions, Henry VIII greatly increased the English monarchy's income. Protestantism brought with it English translations of the Bible, and a Church that was more focused on worshippers' personal relationship with God, rather than ritual and performance. Today, the Church of England remains England's state church. What little remains of England's medieval Catholic history can be seen in the ruined monasteries which haunt the English countryside, such as the magnificent ruins of Whitby Abbey in North Yorkshire (see picture).

Henry VIII is most famous for his six wives. Their varied fates are recalled in the rhyme beloved by English school children: divorced (Catherine of Aragon); beheaded (Anne Boleyn); died (Jane Seymour); divorced (Anne of Cleves); beheaded (Catherine Howard); survived (Catherine Parr). In 1536, Henry VIII was crushed beneath his horse during a jousting tournament. Unable to exercise due to the injuries, Henry VIII's waistline ballooned to a whopping 54 inches (137 centimetres). Henry VIII died in 1547. Over the course of his reign, he had established the Church of England, made himself King of Ireland, invaded France three times, executed both his Lord Chancellor and Chief Minister, and amassed 55 royal palaces. The most magnificent of these was Hampton Court Palace (see picture), located west of London on the River Thames, and given to him by his Lord Chancellor Thomas Wolsey shortly before Wolsey's death.

Henry VIII's third wife, Jane Seymour, did provide Henry VIII with the son he always desired. At the age of nine, he became King Edward VI. However, after just six years on the throne, Edward VI died. The nightmare of an unstable throne with no clear heir had returned to England.

1553 | Mary I and the Counter-Reformation

Following the death of Edward VI, his half-sister Mary became Queen. As the daughter of Catherine of Aragon, Mary was a devout Catholic, who intended to put her father's Protestant Reformation into reverse. The boldness of Mary's plans increased after she married King Philip II of Spain, the most powerful Catholic monarch in Europe. When a knight called Sir Thomas Wyatt led a rebellion against the marriage, he was beheaded and 120 of his supporters were hanged, their bodies left to rot on gallows in their home villages.

Under Mary's Catholic counter-reformation, churches were ordered once again to celebrate Mass and hold services in Latin; the Protestant *Book of Common Prayer* was outlawed; and priests who had married were forced to give up their wives. Those who refused to give up their Protestant faith risked being burnt at the stake, an agonisingly slow and painful death in which victims could feel, see and smell their flesh burn before their eyes. In all, 283 Protestants suffered this fate. However, on 1558 Mary I died childless. After her death, Protestant England turned their last Catholic Queen into a figure of hate: forever remembered as 'Bloody Mary'.

1558 | Elizabeth I

Ruling for forty-four years, Elizabeth I was one of England's greatest monarchs. On being crowned Queen, Elizabeth put an end to three decades of religious turmoil by returning England to Protestantism, whilst tolerating England's remaining Catholic minority. As her advisor, the philosopher and scientist Francis Bacon recorded, she did not want to create 'windows into men's souls'.

Elizabeth ruled with a combination of determination and a steely independent-mindedness. She saw off the two greatest threats to her reign, Mary Queen of Scots (see page 74) and the Spanish Armada (see page 76). Nowhere was Elizabeth's steeliness more apparent than in her decision not to marry. Throughout her reign, her advisors and Parliament were desperate for the Queen to choose a husband, and produce a Protestant heir. However, Elizabeth was wary of the conflict a marriage could cause within her court, and the threat a husband might pose to her own power as Queen. Elizabeth's determination won out, as she famously explained: 'I will have here but one mistress and no master.' The peace and stability of Elizabeth's reign allowed England to flourish, and she died in 1603 loved by her people as the 'Virgin Queen'.

1580 | Sir Francis Drake

The Elizabethan period was an age of sailors and explorers. One of Elizabeth I's favourite courtiers was the dashing Sir Walter Raleigh. Raleigh's journeys to the 'New World' in America helped establish smoking tobacco as a popular pastime in Elizabeth's court, and many suspected Elizabeth I was secretly in love with him.

But the greatest sailor of Elizabethan England has to have been Sir Francis Drake. A tough young sailor from Devon, Drake worked for Queen Elizabeth as a 'privateer' (essentially, a state-sponsored pirate). He would raid Spanish galleons and trade ports around the world, and return to England with their cargos of silver and gold. In an epic journey from 1577–1580, Drake became the first Englishman to circumnavigate the globe in his ship the *Golden Hind*. Having sailed through the treacherous Magellan Strait, Drake captured an unprotected Spanish galleon full of gold off the coast of Peru. When he returned from his voyage, Drake moored the *Golden Hind* in Deptford, and invited the Queen to join him for dinner on board. A replica of the *Golden Hind* can still be seen in Southwark today (see picture).

1587 | Mary Queen of Scots

English Catholics could never accept Elizabeth I as their Queen. Their opposition intensified in 1570 when the Pope denounced Elizabeth I as a heretic, and threatened to excommunicate any English Catholic who remained loyal to her.

Many English Catholics were involved in secret plots to replace Elizabeth I with her Catholic cousin, Mary Queen of Scots (not to be confused with Mary I). Mary Queen of Scots had a claim to the English throne as the great-granddaughter of Henry VII. In 1568, the people of Scotland forced Mary to abdicate her throne, and she fled to England. Elizabeth knew that her Catholic cousin was a serious threat, so she imprisoned Mary for nineteen years in a series of stately homes and castles around England. In 1587, Elizabeth I's spymaster Francis Walsingham discovered that Mary Queen of Scots had been communicating from her prison in Fotheringhay Castle with English Catholics plotting to assassinate Elizabeth. They had been using coded letters, smuggled in and out of prison in waterproof cases used to bung the top of beer barrels. At the urging of her advisors, Elizabeth I ordered the execution of her cousin. Mary was beheaded at Fotheringhay Castle on 8th December 1587.

1588 | The Spanish Armada

King Philip II of Spain longed to see England return to Catholicism. With Mary Queen of Scots executed in 1587, there was little chance of this happening. So, the following year Philip assembled the largest naval invasion force Europe had ever seen to invade England. The Spanish Armada set sail from Lisbon with 130 Spanish galleons and 26,000 men.

The English navy, jointly led by Sir Francis Drake (see page 72), chased the Armada along the English Channel, until it moored beside the French town of Calais on 27th July, waiting for reinforcements. The following night, the English navy filled eight ships with gunpowder and tar (known as 'hellburners'), set them alight and then set them on course for the stationary Spanish Armada. Though the hellburners did not sink any Spanish ships, they did scatter them. The Spanish then made the severe error of trying to escape the English by sailing their Armada around Scotland and Ireland, where they were devastated by fierce storms. Around sixty ships were wrecked off the coasts of Scotland and Ireland, before the defeated Armada finally returned to Spain in early 1589. Elizabeth I's reign had been saved by a combination of good luck and terrible weather.

1590 | Shakespeare

There was such a great flowering of science, philosophy and culture during Elizabeth's reign that it is sometimes termed the 'Golden Age'. No Elizabethan is more celebrated today than William Shakespeare. Between 1590 and 1613, Shakespeare wrote thirty-eight plays including comedies such as *Much Ado About Nothing* and *A Midsummer Night's Dream*, tragedies such as *Hamlet* and *Macbeth*, and histories such as *Henry V* and *Richard III*. Little is known about Shakespeare's life, but he is thought to have gone to a grammar school in Stratford-upon-Avon, before going to London to work as an actor. Many of Shakespeare's plays were first performed in the Globe Theatre. Today, a stunning replica of the Globe Theatre stands on the southern bank of the Thames, a few hundred yards from its original site.

A trip to the theatre was very different during Shakespeare's day. Food and drink were sold in the stalls and there was plenty of interaction between the actors and the audience. Rowdy audiences would cheer, boo and pelt bad performers with food. Elizabeth I enjoyed the theatre, and the best performance in London's public theatres would transfer to be performed at the Royal Court.

1603 | King James VI and I

Elizabeth died with no heir, so the throne passed to her distant relative King James VI of Scotland. James was the son of Mary Queen of Scots, but she was imprisoned in England for almost his entire childhood. For this reason, James was raised in Scotland by Protestant guardians. James I was crowned King of England in 1603, uniting the English and Scottish thrones under the same monarch for the first time in history. But England and Scotland remained two separate countries, with two separate Parliaments.

James I was offered the English throne because he had renounced the Catholic faith of his mother. To affirm his commitment to Protestantism, James authorised a new translation of the Bible into English. A team of forty-seven scholars working in Oxford, Cambridge and Westminster took seven years to complete the task. First published in 1611, the King James Bible remains the most widely published book in the English language. The exquisite poetry of the translation has had a marked effect on the English language. Countless common phrases such as 'writing on the wall' and 'eat, drink and be merry' can be traced back to this landmark literary project.

1605 | The Gunpowder Plot

With the Protestant James I on the English throne, some Catholics believed that only extreme action could achieve their dream of returning England to the 'Old Faith'. In 1604, a Catholic named Robert Catesby began assembling a group of plotters. Their plan was to rent a cellar beneath the Houses of Parliament, and stack it with thirty-six barrels of gunpowder. The fuse would be lit on the morning of 5th November, during the State Opening of Parliament. On this day, the entire governing class of England would assemble in Parliament, including King James I. Had it succeeded, the Gunpowder Plot would have been the most destructive terrorist attack, up to that point in history.

Responsibility for the barrels of gunpowder was given to a battle-hardened mercenary from York called Guy Fawkes. Early in the morning of 5th November, the King's troops were sent to search the cellars below Parliament. Fawkes was caught, arrested, and tortured on the rack until he confessed the location of his fellow plotters. They were rounded up and tried for treason, before being hung, drawn and quartered. Every year on the 5th November communities across England still celebrate 'Bonfire Night', where effigies of Guy Fawkes are burnt on bonfires.

1629 | Charles I and Parliament

James I's son Charles I became King in 1625, and showed a fatal combination of stubbornness and bad judgement. Since Parliament was first established during the 13th century (see page 42), English monarchs were expected to rule alongside their Members of Parliament, to ensure wars and laws had the support of the people. However, Charles I believed that he had been appointed directly by God, and no person had the right to question his power.

From 1629, Charles I did not call Parliament once, a period known as the 'eleven year tyranny'. Charles I resorted to underhand methods such as 'ship money' and 'forced loans' to raise money without Parliament's consent. In addition, Charles's French Catholic wife was despised by English Protestants, and many suspected he was a secret Catholic. Charles's unpopular religious reforms caused war to break out in Scotland, and the King was forced to recall Parliament in 1640. In return for approving new taxes to raise an army, Parliament demanded that Charles work alongside them, but Charles could not agree. By the start of 1642 violent conflict seemed inevitable. Both Parliament and the King began to raise their own armies, and the English Civil War broke out in August 1642.

1642 | The English Civil War

The English Civil War lasted for seven years, and led to an estimated 5 per cent of England's population dying – a higher proportion than died during the First World War. As many as 150 towns saw serious damage, and around 11,000 houses were burned or demolished, including historic stately houses such as Basing House and fortifications like Corfe Castle.

Different parts of England declared for either the Royalist or the Parliamentarian side. The Royalists gained the nickname 'Cavaliers' (taken from the Spanish word for horseman), due to their romantic and often aristocratic cavalrymen. They liked to have long hair and expensive clothing, often going into battle dressed in shirts with ruffled cuffs and beaver hats with ostrich feather plumes. The Parliamentarians earned the nickname 'Roundheads', probably due to the shaved heads of some of their supporters. Their officers were more likely to be recruited from the minor gentry, and were known for their strict discipline and devout Protestantism. What the Cavaliers had in style, the Roundheads had in discipline and conviction. In 1645, the Parliamentarians won a decisive victory against King Charles at the Battle of Naseby, turning the tide of the war in Parliament's favour. By 1647, King Charles I had been taken prisoner by his own Parliament.

1649 | Regicide

Having taken Charles I prisoner, Parliament resumed their negotiations with the King. However, once again, Charles I stubbornly refused to come to any settlement. In November 1647, Charles I escaped from his prison in Hampton Court, and rode to the Isle of Wight. This sparked a second Civil War, which ended in 1648 with a bloody three-day battle in Preston.

Charles I's enemies were running out of patience, particularly the officers in Parliament's army. In December 1648, the Parliamentarian army staged a coup, expelling from Parliament all Members who supported continued negotiations with the King. The remaining MPs now placed King Charles I on trial. His charge? Being 'a tyrant, traitor, murderer and a public and implacable enemy to the commonwealth of England'. Charles refused to answer any of the charges throughout the trial, arguing that it is impossible to try a king for treason. Even if Charles had defended himself, the verdict was not in doubt. Charles I was led to the executioner's block on 30th January 1649. According to witnesses, there was a deathly silence following his beheading. No one in the crowd could quite believe that, for the first time in its history, England was without a monarch.

BANCKET H

With Charles I beheaded, England entered the first and only period of her history as a republic. England was declared a 'Commonwealth', the House of Lords was abolished, and many spoke of living in a 'world turned upside down'. After a few years of Parliament ruling over England, a cavalry General named Oliver Cromwell rose to take full control of the country.

Cromwell was a member of the minor gentry from Huntingdon, near Cambridge. During the 1620s Cromwell converted to Puritanism, a radical form of Protestantism whose followers aimed to live 'pure' lives without greed or sin. Cromwell was famously bluff and direct, but also a brutally effective military leader during the Civil War, and later on campaign in Scotland and Ireland. In 1653, Cromwell dismissed Parliament and made himself 'Lord Protector', a King in all but name. Cromwell imposed his Puritan beliefs on England, making theatre, dancing and pubs illegal. Cromwell even banned Christmas celebrations – which he saw as an ungodly excuse for drunkenness and frivolity. To enforce his rule, Cromwell appointed eleven Major-Generals to govern the different regions of Britain. Cromwell died in 1658, and the grey cloud of Puritanism and military dictatorship began to lift.

1660| Restoration

Following Cromwell's death, it was clear that England's republican experiment was failing. In 1660, Parliament began negotiations with Charles I's son, also called Charles, who had been living in exile since the end of the Civil War. Straightaway, Charles showed more willingness to compromise than his father, and Parliament invited him to return to England.

In May 1660, Charles was cheered into London by ecstatic crowds, as the streets were strewn with flowers, church bells rang, and alcohol flowed freely. The monarchy was restored, and a new period known as the 'Restoration' had begun. Once crowned King, Charles II promised forgiveness for all crimes committed during the English Civil Wars. The only exception were the 59 regicides who signed his father's death warrant, who were sentenced to death. Those (such as Cromwell) who had already died were exhumed so their corpses could be beheaded. Charles II's fun-loving ways lent the Restoration period its culture of hedonism and frivolity. Nicknamed the 'Merry Monarch', Charles II wore magnificent clothes and a wig of curly black hair. He loved drinking, gambling, and dancing, and is known to have fathered at least fourteen children outside of his marriage.

1666 | Great Fire of London

The summer of 1666 was long and hot. By September, London's medieval houses, which were made out of wood and straw, were tinder-box dry. On the night of 2nd September, a baker who lived on Pudding Lane left his ovens on overnight. During the night, the whole bakery went up in flames, and warm winds rapidly spread the fire across the city. By morning, fire was raging through London so quickly that flying pigeons were seen being caught by the flames in mid-flight.

How would the people of London stop the fire? There were no firemen or fire engines, and only the most basic water pumps and hoses. The only solution was to pull down rows and rows of houses in order to create barriers (known as firebreaks) over which the fire could not pass. After four days of destruction, the fire finally stopped on 7th September. In all, the Great Fire claimed 13,200 houses, along with eighty-seven churches, fourty-four merchant guildhalls, and all of the commercial buildings of the City of London. 100,000 Londoners were left homeless. Remarkably, only six Londoners were recorded as having died, though historians now think the real figure was probably much higher.

1687 | Sir Isaac Newton

Historians often write that a 'scientific revolution' took place during the 17th century. Charles II was a keen supporter of scientific research, and in 1662 helped to found the Royal Society for Improving Natural Knowledge. Many great scientists joined the Royal Society, but no scientist had a greater impact than Sir Isaac Newton.

So the story goes, Newton was sitting under a tree when an apple fell on his head. This led him to wonder what forced the apple downwards, and the answer was gravity. Newton realised that all objects attract each other, depending on their mass and distance. This explains not only why an apple falls to the floor, but also why planets orbit the Sun. Newton explained gravity, his three laws of motion, and much more in a book titled *Principia Mathematica*, which was published in 1687. It is often described as the most important book in the history of science. Newton was the first English scientist to be knighted, but he remained modest about his discoveries. Sir Isaac Newton compared himself to a boy playing with pebbles on the seashore, aware that 'the great ocean of truth lay all undiscovered before me.'

1688 | The Glorious Revolution

In 1685, James II was crowned king. He was set on ruling England as an absolute monarch, dismissing Parliament the year that he was crowned. More worrying still for the people of England, James II was a Catholic. When his second wife (who was from Italy) gave birth to a son, this all but guaranteed a Catholic future for the English throne.

England's leading Protestant politicians wrote to a Dutch Protestant Prince named William of Orange (image opposite), who was the grandson of Charles I and was married to James II's daughter Mary. William and Mary were effectively invited to invade England and rid the country of its Catholic King. They duly did so in the autumn of 1688, landing on the Devon coast with an army of 40,000 men. However, no blood was shed in England. Seeing that his support was crumbling, James II abandoned his throne for exile in France. William and Mary were crowned joint King and Queen of England the following year. To ensure they never drifted towards absolutism, William and Mary were made to sign the Bill of Rights, a landmark agreement that limited the power of the English monarchy, and secured the legal and political rights that Parliament still holds today.

1707 | The Act of Union

Queen Anne was England's last Stuart monarch, and her life was cursed with bad luck. Even though she had eighteen children, none of them survived long enough to succeed her. Towards the end of Anne's reign, she and Parliament were greatly concerned about who would succeed her. Her Catholic half-brother James Stuart was living in exile in France, and believed that he should be king. More worrying still, it looked likely that Scotland might choose James Stuart as their new King following Anne's death.

To avoid Scotland choosing a different King to England, Parliament proposed that the two countries should unite, sharing one monarch, with one Parliament based in England. At first, the Scots were deeply opposed to this idea and there was rioting in some Scottish cities. However, the country was on the verge of bankruptcy due to a failed attempt to establish a Scottish colony in Central America. The English Parliament were able to win round the Scottish leaders with some very generous bribes, and the Scottish Parliament voted itself into non-existence. On 1st May 1707, a new nation was born: Great Britain. A flag was designed to represent the union between England and Scotland, which combined the cross of St Andrew and the cross of St George. It was nicknamed the Union Jack.

1714 | The House of Hanover

Queen Anne died in 1714. The Act of Settlement of 1701 stated that only a Protestant monarch was permitted to succeed her, so the throne had to pass to Anne's closest surviving Protestant relative. The answer was found in the shape of George Ludwig, the fifty-four-year-old ruler of a small German state called Hanover. George just happened to be the great-grandson of James I.

George Ludwig arrived in London on 18th September with a procession of 260 horse-drawn carriages, and was crowned King George I of Great Britain a month later. Britain now had a new royal family, known as the Hanoverians. For many people, it was a strange development. There were fifty-seven Catholic descendants of the Stuarts across Europe with a better claim to the throne than George I. Before being plucked from obscurity to become King of Great Britain, George I had only visited England once. He spoke no English and took little interest in the country, preferring to spend his time playing cards, visiting Germany, and entertaining his two mistresses. Parliament's power over the government of Britain had been steadily increasing, so the arrival of a foreign king, indifferent to much of what was happening in the country he ruled, suited them rather well.

1721 | Britain's first Prime Minister

Having spent all his life in Germany, King George I knew almost nothing about how to rule Britain. For this reason, he was heavily reliant on government ministers. One such minister was Robert Walpole. A wealthy farmer from Norfolk and a Member of Parliament, Robert Walpole weighed twenty stone, loved drinking and eating, and was very ambitious. Walpole's political career took off after an economic crash called the South Sea Bubble devastated Britain's economy. He successfully restored Britain's economy, and in the process Walpole became George I's favourite minister.

In 1721, Walpole was given three of the key jobs in British politics: First Lord of the Treasury, Chancellor of the Exchequer and Leader of the House of Commons. This made him the most important minister in the King's government, so people would refer to him as the 'prime' minister. The king gave him a house in London to live in, and selected number 10 on a new development near Parliament called 'Downing Street'. Walpole recommended that the house should forever remain the property of whoever held his position. To this day the Prime Minister of Great Britain lives at 10 Downing Street.

1739 | Highwaymen

During the 1700s, Britain saw an increase in highwaymen: armed robbers on horseback who attacked people in stagecoaches as they travelled along dark, empty roads. The use of cheques only became common during the second half of the century, so travellers often had to carry large sums of money in person. Travellers came to dread the sound of galloping hooves and pistol shots, followed by the infamous highwayman cry: 'Stand and Deliver! Your money or your life!'

Highwaymen had their origin in the aftermath of the English Civil War. Following the execution of Charles I, many Royalist cavalrymen lost their livelihoods, so turned to highway robbery as a source of income. This 'gentlemanly' origin leant the highwayman a romantic air, and highwaymen were said to show impeccable manners whilst relieving travellers of their money. The most famous such highwayman was Dick Turpin. Today, he is remembered as a dashing hero with his beloved stallion Black Bess, but this characterisation is the result of a romanticised Victorian novel. In reality, Dick Turpin was a brutal thief, who terrorised the roads and farmhouses of Essex, before being caught and executed at York racecourse in 1739.

1740 | Rule, Britannia!

From the early 1600s onwards, Britain began to establish overseas colonies. In the 'New World' of North America, British settlers developed sugar plantations on Caribbean islands, cotton and tobacco plantations in the south of the continent, and the Puritan settlements in the North. In India, the East India Company developed a series of coastal trading posts such as Bombay, Madras and Calcutta. Nothing better sums up the confidence and pride that Britain had developed in its Empire by the 18th century than *Rule, Britannia!*, first performed in 1740.

The British Empire began as a trading Empire, and rapidly transformed Britain into a consumer society. Goods from Britain's overseas colonies such as tobacco and sugar, which had once been seen as luxuries, fast became necessities. At the beginning of the 18th century, people from a modest background would have dressed exclusively in linen and woollen cloth. By the end of the 18th century, a woman could wear fine cotton textiles or Chinese silk, while her husband could wear a fashionable tricorn hat made from Canadian beaver fur. Ports such as London, Bristol, Liverpool and Glasgow, which received cargo from Britain's colonies around the world, became the country's fastest growing cities. The image opposite is of St Katharine Docks, London.

1745 | Jacobite uprising

During the 1700s, 'Jacobites' retained a passionate belief that the Stuart royal family should still be governing Britain instead of the Hanoverians (see page 100). Charles Edward Stuart was the eldest son of James Stuart, the self-styled King James III of Great Britain. In 1745 he set sail for Great Britain, hoping to start a Jacobite uprising against the Hanoverian King George II, which would return the throne to his father.

Charles began his rebellion in Glenfinnan (see picture) in the Scottish Highlands where support for the Jacobite cause was strongest. Nicknamed 'Bonnie Prince Charlie' by his Scottish followers thanks to his boyish good looks, Charles took Scotland with ease. By November, Bonnie Prince Charlie was marching his army of 6,000 men south towards London. However, the Jacobites only made it as far as Derby before turning back to Scotland. By the spring of 1746, George II had raised an army to defeat Prince Charlie. They met for a final battle at Culloden Moor, near Inverness, in April, where the Jacobite army was devastated by the British cannons and cavalry. The Stuart cause was dead, and the Hanoverians were safely established as Britain's royal family. Culloden remains the last battle ever to be fought on British soil.

1755 | Dr Johnson's Dictionary

The son of a poor bookseller from Lichfield, Samuel Johnson's childhood was plagued with illness. However, he showed remarkable intellectual ability, and at the age of nineteen Johnson entered Pembroke College, Oxford. Due to a lack of funds, Johnson was unable to complete his degree, so he returned to Lichfield. After a failed attempted to set up a school, Johnson walked to London to make a career as a writer.

Johnson saw some success as a critic and poet, but his big break came when he was commissioned to write a dictionary of the English language. After almost ten years of work, Johnson's dictionary was published in 1755. It contained definitions for 40,000 words. These included some famously amusing entries. Johnson defined 'oats' as 'a grain, which in England is generally given to horses, but in Scotland supports the people.' He defined 'dull' as 'Not exhilarating; not delightful; as, to make dictionaries is dull work.' Johnson was famously overweight and ugly, and he had lots of nervous tics. However, because he was so witty and intelligent, his company was highly sought after by Georgian high society, in particular his lifelong friend and biographer James Boswell.

1763 | The Seven Years War

By the mid-18th century, Britain's trade routes and power spread across the world. However, it had a great rival in its project to build a global Empire: France. This rivalry spilled over into war in 1756. The Seven Years War was the world's first truly global conflict. In 1759, Britain won a series of significant victories. A British army under the command of General Wolfe took Quebec, the capital of French possessions in North America, and the Royal Navy defeated the French at the Battle of Quiberon Bay. Meanwhile, the victory of Robert Clive over the French-supported Nawab of Bengal in 1757 set the stage for Britain's expansion into India.

When Britain signed the Treaty of Paris with France in 1763, Britain had expanded its power in India, taken control of most of North America, gained French islands in the Caribbean, and kept control of Gibraltar and Minorca in the Mediterranean. The end of the Seven Years War marked the beginning of the British Empire's global dominance, which would last for another 150 years. The words of *Rule Britannia!* (see page 106), first performed two decades previously, seemed to be coming true: 'Rule Britannia! Britannia rules the waves.'

1700s | Food and Empire

The British Empire changed how English people ate and drank. Many dishes which are today seen as quintessentially English in fact have their origin half way around the world. The amount of tea that the East India Company imported from China increased from 1 million kg in 1720 to 14.5 million kg in 1790. Though tea is drunk on its own in China, the British took to combining it with milk and sugar, creating a national drink that remains as popular as it ever was. The wealthy took their tea in finely made white porcelain imported from China, which was prized for its thinness. This porcelain became known, unsurprisingly, as 'china'.

Spices from India and the Far East such as ginger, nutmeg and cinnamon were used to create more typically 'English' dishes such as cakes, spiced buns and chutneys (taken from the Indian word *chatni*). By the end of the 18th century, an English writer estimated that workers in southern England were spending 11 per cent of their wages on sugar, treacle and tea. But there was a shameful secret that lay behind all of this cheerful consumption: Britain's buoyant trade in consumer goods was built on the enslavement of Africans.

1770 | Captain Cook and Australia

On 26th August 1768, naval captain James Cook was sent on a scientific expedition to observe the transit of Venus in Tahiti, on board his ship the *Endeavour*. Also part of Cook's mission was to search for and claim for Britain a mysterious continent in the South Pacific Ocean known as *Terra Australis*, Latin for 'Southern land'. Despite almost sinking the *Endeavour* when he ran aground on the Great Barrier Reef, Captain Cook claimed Australia for King George III on 22nd August 1770. Cook never returned to Australia. During his third great Pacific voyage, Cook landed on the island of Hawaii in 1779. Here, relations with the native islanders turned sour, and Captain Cook was clubbed to death.

Meanwhile, Parliament decided that Britain should use the newly discovered island of Australia as a prison, and the first British convicts were sent there in 1788. Many of these convicts chose to stay in Australia having served their sentences, and became the first European settlers on the island. British settlers in Australia devastated the population of indigenous people, known as Aborigines. It has been estimated that between 1788 and 1900, Australia's Aboriginal population decreased by 90 per cent, as a result of diseases imported by the arrival of Europeans.

1772 | The Slave Trade

By the mid-17th century, Britain's growing American and Caribbean plantations needed workers. The answer lay in transporting slaves from Africa. It has been estimated that between 1640 and 1807, British merchants transported 3.1 million slaves across the Atlantic, 2.7 million of whom survived. It took two to three months for a slave ship to reach America from West Africa, and the African captives were transported in conditions of unimaginable cruelty (see picture). They were stacked lengthways on wooden shelves and kept in place with chains, developing open wounds as their arms and legs rubbed against their shackles. Unable to move, the slaves became surrounded by vomit, excrement and urine.

The wealth of British cities such as Liverpool and Bristol came to depend on the Slave Trade. Rich slave owners returned to Britain with their fortunes and built magnificent country houses and art collections, which now sit in our national galleries. By the late 1700s, Britain had developed a small population of African freemen and slaves, particularly in ports such as London and Liverpool. In 1772 it was ruled that slavery was unsupported by English law, but it would take another sixty years for slavery to be abolished throughout the British Empire.

PLAN OF LOWER DECK WITH THE STOWAGE OF 292 SLAVES

130 OF THESE BEING STOWED UNDER THE SHELVES AS SHEWN IN FIGURE D & FIGURE 5.

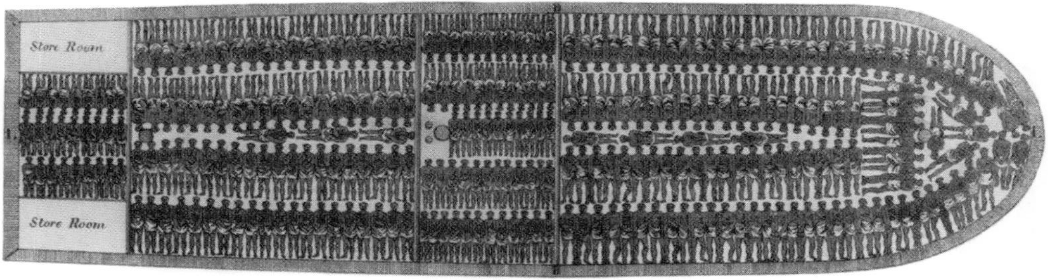

Store Room.

Store Room.

Fig 2

1775 | Britain's first factories

Before the Industrial Revolution, all manufactured goods were made by hand. Today, almost all goods we purchase are produced by machines. The first product in Britain to make this transition was cotton textiles, due to a series of inventions during the late 1700s. The first was James Hargreaves 'spinning jenny', a hand-powered machine that could spin raw cotton into multiple thin cotton threads at once. The next breakthrough came when a Bolton wig maker called Richard Arkwright invented a cotton-spinning machine powered by water.

Richard Arkwright was a shrewd businessman. In 1775, Arkwright opened a five-storey water mill beside the Derwent River in Cromford, Derbyshire, to spin cotton. The Cromford Mill went on to employ 800 people, and many claim it was the world's first modern factory. In 1785, one of Boulton and Watt's newly invented steam engines (see page 122) was used to power a cotton spinning machine for the first time. This meant that coal-powered cotton mills could be built in urban areas such as Manchester. Due to cotton manufacturing, Manchester grew from a small market town of 10,000 people in 1720, to a world city of 380,000 people in 1860, earning Manchester the nickname 'Cottonopolis'. The image opposite is of an old cotton mill in Manchester.

1776 | American Revolution

By the late 1700s, Britain's territories in North America had grown to cover thirteen colonies along the Eastern seaboard, with a population of around 2.4 million people. At first, the British government gave the American colonies a large degree of freedom to govern themselves. However, following the Seven Years War (see page 112) Britain tried to exert more control, in particular through increased taxation. The American colonists were furious, demanding that there should be 'no taxation without representation'.

Delegates from each of the thirteen colonies formed a 'Congress' to decide what to do, and in 1776 Congress voted for complete independence from Britain. One delegate named Thomas Jefferson wrote a formal Declaration of Independence, which Congress approved on 4th July 1776. Back in Britain, King George III and Parliament refused to accept American independence, so they sent an army of 32,000 troops to defeat the rebel colonists. After many years of fierce fighting, the British army surrendered at the Battle of Yorktown in 1781. A band of rebel colonists had stood up to the largest Empire in the world, and won. King George III was left humiliated, and the United States of America was born.

1776 | Steam engine

For the whole of its history up until the 18th century, humankind had depended upon the natural world for power. James Watt was a Scottish engineer who set himself the challenge of finding an alternative. In 1764, he started work on an engine that would convert fossil fuels into power by heating water, and using the steam to power pistons. Watt struggled to make his steam engine work, so in 1774 he moved to Birmingham, to become business partners with a wealthy factory owner called Matthew Boulton. Their partnership prospered, and two years later Boulton and Watt built their first two functioning steam engines. One was used to pump water out of a coalmine, the other was used to power bellows for a blast furnace.

Over the course of the 19th century, the power created by steam engines was harnessed to weave textiles, harvest wheat, power trains, print newspapers, and eventually create electricity. By unlocking the energy within fossil fuels, James Watt's steam engine liberated humankind from its dependence on wind, water and muscle as sources of power. More than any other invention, the steam engine created the Industrial Revolution, and consequently the world that we inhabit today.

1788 | Mad King George

Crowned in 1760, George III (image opposite) was the first Hanoverian king to have been born and brought up in England. He declared during the first Parliament of his reign: 'I glory in the name of Briton'. King George III was very popular amongst the British people, despite his role in the loss of the American colonies (see page 120).

However, from 1788 the King began to exhibit some concerning behaviour. George III would speak for several hours without stopping, causing him to foam at the mouth, and he suffered from convulsions so violent that his attendants had to pin him to the floor. In an attempt to cure his madness, the King's doctors would shave and burn his scalp, or apply leeches to his forehead to draw the poison from his brain. Other times, he was simply confined to a straitjacket and left in a cold empty room. For the last ten years of his reign, George III was incapable of ruling, so his authority passed to his son (the future George IV), who ruled as Prince Regent. Though not mad, George IV was notoriously debauched. The Prince Regent's continuous drinking and gambling began to turn many of his subjects against the British monarchy.

1791 | *Rights of Man*

Thomas Paine was the son of a Norfolk corset maker, who emigrated to America two years before the colonists declared independence from British rule (see page 120). During the American Revolution, Paine worked as a political pamphleteer, and played an important role in inspiring the American colonists towards supporting independence. In 1789, Paine found himself back in England as another popular revolt against monarchical power was underway – the French Revolution.

Paine was a fervent supporter of the French Revolution, and wrote a defence of it in 1791 titled *Rights of Man*. The book was decades ahead of its time, criticising monarchy, aristocracy and organised religion, and calling for public education, old-age pensions, and a progressive income tax. *Rights of Man* sold in the tens of thousands, and Paine was invited to France to join the revolution. The following year, the writer Mary Wollstonecraft published *Vindication of the Rights of Women*, arguing that not only should men be entitled to basic rights, so too should women. Wollstonecraft argued that if women were offered the same education and upbringing as men, they would be capable of pursing the same opportunities in society – an idea even further ahead of its time than Thomas Paine's.

1805 | The Battle of Trafalgar

Out of the chaos that followed the French Revolution, Napoleon Bonaparte rose to become the Emperor of the French. Napoleon's rise to power was staggering, and much of Europe fell under his control. In 1803, Napoleon began plans to invade Britain, and assembled an army of around 165,000 men on the channel coast. However, Napoleon knew that before his army could invade Britain, he first had to defeat the Royal Navy.

In September 1805, Britain sent their best admiral, Horatio Nelson, to defeat the joint French and Spanish fleet. Battle-hardened and famously fearless, Nelson had already lost an eye and an arm in combat. He engaged the French and Spanish off the Cape of Trafalgar in southern Spain, and won a resounding victory on 21st October. As the battle came to an end, Admiral Nelson was shot by a French sniper, and died below deck on his ship the HMS *Victory*. Nelson lived just long enough to know that the Franco/Spanish fleet had been defeated, guaranteeing that Napoleon could no longer launch an invasion of Britain. In 1840, a monument was built to commemorate Lord Nelson, and today his column still stands in the middle of Trafalgar Square in central London.

1813 | Jane Austen

No writer captured the life of the English gentry during the reign of George III as well as Jane Austen. The gentry were England's wealthy middle class – one step below the aristocracy, but still able to enjoy a lifestyle of grand estates, elegant balls and country sports. It was into the lower rungs of the gentry that Jane Austen was born in 1775, the seventh child of a village rector. Austen's father encouraged his daughters to gain an education, and Jane showed remarkable early promise as a writer.

In 1813, Austen published her most famous novel *Pride and Prejudice*. It follows the story of Elizabeth Bennet, an intelligent and witty young woman who falls in love with a wealthy but aloof landowner called Mr Darcy. Like all of Austen's work, *Pride and Prejudice* subtly mocked the manners and concerns of the English gentry, in particular their willingness to marry for social advancement. Austen's books were published anonymously during her lifetime, as was the convention for female authors. She died in 1817 aged only 41, but her reputation continued to grow. In 1833, the collected edition of Jane Austen's works was published. Her novels have never been out of print since.

1815 | Duke of Wellington

In 1815, Napoleon Bonaparte made one last attempt to defeat his European enemies. In response, the Duke of Wellington was given command to lead an allied army (including British, Dutch, Belgian and German troops) against the French. The two armies met outside the Belgian village of Waterloo on 18th June 1815. The Battle of Waterloo was hard fought, lasting for eleven hours, and was only won late in the afternoon when a Prussian army arrived to reinforce Wellington's troops. Napoleon was conclusively defeated, but the cost in human lives was high. When asked about the victory later in life, the Duke of Wellington said, 'It is quite impossible to think of glory...Next to a battle lost, the greatest misery is a battle gained.'

Following Waterloo, Napoleon turned himself over to the British, and was imprisoned for the rest of his life on a rocky volcanic island in the middle of the South Atlantic Ocean called St Helena. The Duke of Wellington's place as one of Britain's greatest ever military leaders was confirmed. He went on to a career in politics, serving as a Tory Prime Minister from 1828 to 1830, during which his trenchantly conservative views earned Wellington the nickname the 'Iron Duke'.

1829 | The Metropolitan Police Force

Throughout history, urbanisation has been associated with increases in crime and social disorder. Britain in the 19th century was no different. Crime was a growing public concern in Britain's rapidly growing industrial towns, so a young Home Secretary called Robert Peel took action. In 1829, Peel passed the Metropolitan Police Act, establishing a force of 1,000 full-time London policemen. London already had around 450 unpaid parish constables, but they were too disorganised and few in number to cope with the city's crime. In contrast, the Metropolitan Police were centrally managed from a head office in Whitehall called Scotland Yard.

Metropolitan Police constables had to be over 5 foot 7 inches (1.7 metres), and were given a uniform of blue tailcoat, belt, and a metal-lined top hat. Their tailcoats had stiff collars, designed to prevent the officers from being strangled. Peel insisted that the Metropolitan Police should not be seen as a military force, so they were armed with truncheons instead of guns. Policemen were soon nicknamed 'bobbies', or 'peelers', in honour of their founder. Robert Peel went on to be a controversial Prime Minster, whose stance on free trade led to the development of the modern Conservative Party.

1830 | The Railway Age

Following the invention of Boulton and Watt's steam engines (see page 122), many engineers set to work on working out how to attach an engine to a cart on waggonways, so that it could drive itself forward. As early as 1804 Richard Trewithick had designed and built a locomotive that pulled ten tons of iron and 70 men from Cyfarthfa ironworks to Abercynon.

In 1829, a group of Liverpool and Manchester industrialists ran a competition for engineers to design a locomotive capable of travelling between their two cities for commercial purposes. The winner was a locomotive designed by the brilliant self-taught engineer George Stephenson called the *Rocket*, which reached a top speed of 30 miles per hour.

On 15th September 1830, the Liverpool to Manchester Railway opened: it was the first steam-operated passenger service in the world. Around 800 people boarded the inaugural train with enormous excitement, including the Prime Minister, the Duke of Wellington.

For the next twenty years, Britain went through a period known as Railway Mania, as private companies competed to build railway lines across the country. By 1850, 6,100 miles of railway track had been laid, rising to 14,510 miles by 1875. Soon, every major town and city in Britain was connected by rail. The train revolutionised daily life in Victorian Britain, and people began talking about living through the 'Railway Age'.

1833 | Child labour

In industrial areas during the early 19th century, the average age for a child to be sent to work was eight-and-a-half. Some children started work as young as five. In cotton mills (see page 118), children worked as scavengers, crawling beneath the spinning mules to collect loose cotton. Children had to work right next to moving machinery, and if their arms or legs got caught, they could lose a limb. The strain of this physical labour on children's developing bodies caused stunted growth and lifelong deformities, such as knock-knees or a bent spine. Children also worked as chimney sweeps or in coalmines, dragging heavy carts through seams too narrow for adults to access.

By 1830, support was growing in Parliament for factory reform. A Tory aristocrat called Anthony Ashley Cooper, the 7th Earl of Shaftesbury, became its champion. Parliamentary committees were established to investigate child labour in factories, and they uncovered horrific stories of cruelty and abuse. In 1833, Parliament passed the Factory Act, making it illegal for textile factories to employ children under the age of nine. Many more Factory Acts were passed throughout the Victorian period, placing further limits on child labour and working hours.

1833 | Abolition of the Slave Trade

From the 1780s, a growing number of British people started to realise the inhumanity of slavery. Abolitionist campaigners hoped that by raising awareness amongst British people about slavery's cruelty, they could place pressure on Parliament to outlaw the trade. An evangelical Christian named Thomas Clarkson led the abolitionist campaign with enormous energy, claiming to have ridden 35,000 miles in seven years to build support across the country. Clarkson collected objects used by slave traders, such as shackles, whips and branding irons, which he displayed to shocked audiences in public talks.

Abolitionists sent anti-slavery petitions signed by millions of British people to Parliament, and organised consumer boycotts of slave-produced sugar from the West Indies. Former slaves joined the movement, and some such as Olaudah Equiano wrote memoirs detailing their horrific experience of enslavement. The abolitionist cause gained support in Parliament from another evangelical Christian, William Wilberforce. After decades of campaigning, Parliament outlawed the Transatlantic Slave Trade in 1807. It was not until 1833 that slavery itself was abolished throughout the British Empire. One month before Parliament passed the Slavery Abolition Act, William Wilberforce – who had dedicated his life to this cause – died aged 73.

AM I NOT A MAN AND A BROTHER?

1837 | Queen Victoria

Queen Victoria inherited the throne from her uncle William IV in 1837. She was eighteen years old, and stood at 4 foot 11 inches (1.5 metres). In 1840, Queen Victoria married her first cousin, a German prince named Albert. Victoria and Albert loved each other deeply, and they had nine children together over the next seventeen years. However, tragedy struck in 1861 when Prince Albert died aged just forty-two. Queen Victoria was paralysed by grief, and disappeared from public life for the next ten years, becoming nicknamed the 'widow of Windsor'.

Queen Victoria slowly returned to public life during the 1870s. She was reinvigorated by her responsibilities as Queen, and took a particular interest in the British Empire. By the end of the 19th century, Victoria had come to symbolise Britain and its Empire, a living embodiment of Britannia. Across the world, hospitals, universities, cities, waterfalls and entire provinces still bear her name. Queen Victoria's influence on public life was so great that the character and outlook of 19th-century Britain – from its emphasis on moral uprightness to its confidence in Empire and belief in progress – became known as 'Victorian'.

1846 | The workhouse

'Please sir, I want some more.' These words, uttered by a poor and starving Oliver Twist to the workhouse master, are some of the most famous in English literature. Workhouses spread across England following the 1834 Poor Law Amendment Act. This Act forced the poor and unemployed to seek relief in 'workhouses', where they would work in return for shelter and food. However, to discourage the poor from claiming relief in workhouses, conditions were deliberately made unpleasant. Families were split up, with different areas for men, women and children. Inmates had to sleep in large dormitories, and wear prison-style uniforms. Work consisted of hard, menial jobs such as breaking stones.

The Victorian poor lived in constant fear that misfortune might land them in the workhouse. In 1846, a scandal emerged from the Andover workhouse. The workhouse master was a former army sergeant and violent drunk, who sold the workhouse food and left its inmates starving. Inmates were made to crush bones to make fertiliser, and were found trying to feed themselves by sucking rotting marrow from inside the bones. Despite such scandals, workhouses continued to operate, and were only formally abolished in 1930.

1851 | Industrial cities

Britain's 1851 census revealed that – for the first time in the country's history – over half the population lived in a town or a city. The growth of Britain's cities was driven by industrialisation, and its speed was staggering. London grew from one million people in 1810, to seven million people by 1911 – making it the largest city in the world. Outside of London, Britain's largest cities had once been medieval trading centres such as York and Norwich, but they were overtaken by industrial centres such as Manchester and Birmingham. Some towns grew out of nothing. Middlesbrough was a small farming village of twenty-five people in 1801. It then began producing iron and steel, and by 1861 it was a large town of 19,000 inhabitants.

As labourers flocked from rural villages to industrial towns, the supply of houses could not keep up with demand. Many families ended up living in conditions of severe overcrowding, often sharing a single room. In some industrial cities, a whole street of houses had to share a single water pump and toilet. A campaign to improve public health led Parliament to intervene, making it mandatory for town councils to provide all housing with sewers, drainage and running water.

1851 | The Great Exhibition

Queen Victoria's husband Prince Albert (see page 142) was greatly interested in the technological changes created by the Industrial Revolution. In 1851, Prince Albert helped to organise an international exhibition celebrating industry and manufacturing. Called 'The Great Exhibition', it contained 100,000 different exhibits from around the world, including a folding piano, the world's largest diamond, and early prototypes of the bicycle and typewriter. Six million people visited the exhibition from Britain and abroad, many taking day trips to London along newly-built railway lines. On 1st May 1851, Queen Victoria opened the exhibition. She recorded in her diary, 'This day is one of the greatest and most glorious of our lives'.

The Great Exhibition was housed in a temporary building constructed from a cast-iron frame and 294,000 panes of glass. Called the 'Crystal Palace', it was the largest glass structure ever built. After the Great Exhibition finished, the Crystal Palace was reassembled on Penge Common in South London, where it stood until it was destroyed by a fire in 1936. But its memory lives on today in the name of Crystal Palace F.C., whose original stadium lay inside the Palace grounds.

1854 | Florence Nightingale

Florence Nightingale's decision to become a nurse aged twenty-four shocked her wealthy upper-class family. Nursing was not seen as a 'respectable' profession, but Nightingale believed she had a calling from God to help the needy. In October 1854, Nightingale read about the dire medical conditions that wounded British soldiers were suffering in the Crimean War. Nightingale travelled to modern-day Turkey with a group of thirty-eight nurses and set about transforming the British military hospital, insisting on good hygiene, clean uniforms and orderly working conditions. The death rate in the hospital dropped from 42 per cent to 2 per cent. Nightingale's fame grew, and the image of her doing night-time rounds to check on wounded soldiers earnt her the nickname 'the Lady of the Lamp'.

Back home in England, Nightingale established the first professional training school for nurses in 1860, and published over 200 books, reports and pamphlets on nursing and hospital design. Today, Nightingale is widely credited with having transformed nursing into a modern profession. All new nurses still take the Nightingale pledge, and the Florence Nightingale Medal is the highest international distinction a nurse can achieve.

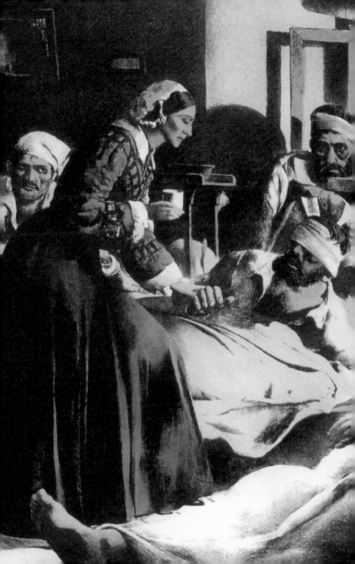

1859 | *On the Origin of Species*

It was during a five-year voyage around the globe that the scientist Charles Darwin first began formulating his theory of natural selection. Whilst on board HMS *Beagle*, Darwin saw how different life forms had adapted to suit different environments, most notably on the Galapagos Islands off the coast of South America, where the same type of songbird differed from island to island. On his return to England in 1836, Charles Darwin began formulating his idea that animals best suited to their environment are more likely to breed, allowing their species to evolve.

Darwin's theory meant that instead of God creating mankind in a single day, mankind had evolved through gradual changes over thousands of years, giving humans common ancestors with other lifeforms such as apes. Darwin was raised a Christian, and had even as a young man studied to become a clergyman. He found his own idea deeply shocking, once telling a friend that 'It is like confessing to a murder'. However, after twenty years of research and writing, Darwin finally published *On the Origin of Species* in November 1859. Darwin's masterpiece revolutionised humankind's understanding of their own history, and has never been out of print since. The photograph opposite shows two marine iguanas which are found on the Galapagos Islands.

1859 | Brunel

Isambard Kingdom Brunel was the most prolific engineer of the Railway Age. Over his career, he designed and built railway lines, railway stations, bridges, tunnels, dockyards and steamships. Brunel's work ethic was intense: he slept only four hours a night, and smoked forty cigars a day. Aged only twenty-seven, Brunel began work on the Great Western Railway (GWR) line from London to Bristol. To keep the GWR direct, Brunel used charges of dynamite to blow a tunnel beneath Box Hill in the Cotswolds. Many railway labourers (known as 'navigators' or 'navvies') died in the construction of Brunel's tunnel, but when it was finished the Box Hill tunnel was the longest in the world. The GWR's construction was so magnificent, that it was nicknamed 'God's Wonderful Railway'.

Later in his career, Brunel turned his mind to building transatlantic steamships, but his ambition was also his downfall. In 1853, Brunel began work on the SS *Great Eastern*, a gargantuan steamship that remained the longest in the world for the next forty years. It left its builders bankrupt, and suffered an explosion on its maiden voyage. Exhausted from his work, Brunel died two weeks after the *Great Eastern's* launch in 1859.

1859 | Big Ben

The English Parliament is one of the oldest in the world, and has been meeting in its current location in Westminster since the 13th century (see page 42). During the medieval period, the Palace of Westminster was the principal residence of the English monarchy, and the traditional meeting place for Parliament. When Henry VIII moved the royal residence to Whitehall Palace, Westminster became Parliament's permanent home. However, in 1834 a fire swept through Westminster, burning almost the entire medieval Palace to the ground.

The celebrated Victorian architect Charles Barry was given the role of designing Britain's new Houses of Parliament. Barry chose to rebuild Parliament in the ornate Gothic Revival style, inspired by the architecture of Medieval England. In 1859, the clock tower in the new Palace of Westminster was completed, and it contained the largest bell ever constructed in England. Nicknamed 'Big Ben' (for reasons unknown), its quarter hourly toll is a distinctive sound of central London. Officially renamed the Elizabeth Tower in 2012 to mark the Diamond Jubilee of Queen Elizabeth II, Big Ben is now one of London's most recognisable landmarks.

1863 | Association Football

Different forms of football had been played around the world for centuries. However, in Victorian England an increasing number of amateur football clubs were being formed by neighbourhoods, factories, schools and universities. These football clubs wanted to compete against each other fairly, but a lack of commonly accepted rules led to disputes. To overcome these disputes, Ebenezer Morley (a London solicitor and captain of Barnes F.C. in South West London) organised a meeting of different football clubs at the Freemasons' Tavern in London on 26th October 1863. The representatives from these clubs called themselves the Football Association, or FA for short.

The FA developed the first comprehensive set of rules of the game, but they were different from the rules we know today: goalkeepers, penalties, corner-kicks and referees were all yet to be created. Passing was not encouraged, and teams often played with six or seven players up front! At first, the Football Association met with limited success, but that all changed in 1871 when they had the idea of organising a knock-out competition, called the FA Cup. Football clubs flocked to take part in the FA Cup, and the Football Association's rules were set on their course for global domination.

1870 | Charles Dickens

There are few English novelists more popular and acclaimed than Charles Dickens, whose novels remain inseparable from the popular image of Victorian England. Born the second of eight children, Dickens's childhood was defined by his parents' financial struggles. They moved around the south of England, living in Portsmouth, Kent and London. Aged twelve, Dickens's father was sent to debtors' prison, and Dickens was forced to leave school and work in a factory sticking labels on bottles – an experience that greatly influenced his later work as a novelist.

At the age of 20, Dickens began work as a journalist. Seven years later, he published his first novel – the wildly successful story of a workhouse orphan named *Oliver Twist*. Dickens went on to write fourteen more novels, as well as hundreds of short stories and pieces of journalism. His novels, such as *Great Expectations*, *Bleak House* and *A Christmas Carol* achieved international success, and Dickens twice went on reading tours to the United States. Dickens died in 1870 to widespread national mourning. His funeral epitaph read: '[Dickens] was a sympathiser with the poor, the suffering, and the oppressed; and by his death, one of England's greatest writers is lost to the world.'

1888 | Jack the Ripper

Whitechapel in East London was notorious during the Victorian period for poverty and overcrowding, and also for crime – none more so than that of the serial killer Jack the Ripper. At 3.40 on the morning of Friday 31st August 1888, the body of Mary Ann Nichols was found on Buck's Row, Whitechapel, her corpse horribly mutilated. A week later another woman's body was found, again mutilated. Three more women were found in similar conditions between September and November. London was thrown into panic, as the Metropolitan Police based in Scotland Yard worked desperately to identify the killer.

On 29th September, Scotland Yard received a letter boasting about the murders, and threatening more to come. It was signed 'Jack the Ripper'. The killer now had a name, but the police were unable to track him down, and the identity of Jack the Ripper remains a mystery. Many amateur detectives known as 'Ripperoligists' still try to solve the mystery to this day. Some suggest that the Ripper must have been a doctor or butcher, based on the precision of the mutilations. Others have suggested prominent public figures, such as Queen Victoria's own grandson Albert Victor, though this claim is now discredited.

1899 | The Boer War

The British Empire gained Cape Colony (now South Africa) from the Dutch in 1814, and with it came a population of 27,000 descendants of Dutch settlers, known as Boers. The Boers were fiercely independent farmers, and they established two independent Boer states within Cape Colony. At first, the British were willing to respect the Boer's territories and freedom, but this all changed in 1866, when diamonds were discovered on a Boer farm. Soon, tens of thousands of British settlers were travelling to the independent Boer states to mine for diamonds, and later gold.

With such great wealth on offer, Britain now wanted to expand its authority into the Boer states, but the tough Boer farmers proved extremely difficult to defeat. Under the command of Lord Kitchener, the British Army destroyed Boer villages, burnt their crops, killed their cattle, and prevented their movement with enormous barbed wire fences. Boer families who had lost their homes were housed in new settlements, which became known as concentration camps. Conditions in the concentration camps were dreadful, leading to the deaths of 25,000 Boers, and 12,000 Africans. Britain won the Boer War in 1902, but at great cost to the British Empire's reputation at home and abroad.

1912 | *Titanic*

When the *Titanic* embarked on her maiden voyage
from Southampton in April 1912, she was the largest
ship in the world. On board were an estimated 2,240
passengers and crew, including a crop of Edwardian
England's industrialists, dignitaries and celebrities.
The *Titanic's* owners promised her passengers that the
Titanic was 'unsinkable', thanks to its state-of-the-art
watertight compartments.

After four days at sea, the *Titanic* was steaming at full speed.
The ship's Captain received reports of ice from other ships,
but he took little heed of the warnings. Then at around
11.30 p.m., a lookout sighted an iceberg. The *Titanic*
grazed the side of the berg, slicing a 90-metre gash in
the ship's hull. In the panic that ensued, women and
children were given priority for boarding the lifeboats,
because the *Titanic* only carried enough lifeboats to save
fewer than half of those on board. After just under three
hours, the *Titanic* had sunk below the Atlantic Ocean.
Only 706 passengers survived, with more than twice that
number meeting their deaths in the icy water. Today, the
Titanic is remembered as a cautionary tale against
excessive ambition: the unsinkable ship that went down
on its maiden voyage.

1913 | Emily Davison

Towards the end of the 19th century, campaigners began to demand that women be granted the same right to vote in elections as men. The leading campaign group was the Suffragists, led by Millicent Fawcett (whose sister, Elizabeth Garrett Anderson, was the first woman in Britain to qualify as a doctor). Formed in 1897, the Suffragists pursued peaceful tactics, such as demonstrations and petitions. However, after many years of national campaigns, Parliament was still unwilling to support the Suffragists' cause. This caused a new more militant group to emerge, called the Suffragettes. The Suffragettes believed nationwide attention would only be captured by radical acts, such as arson, hunger strikes, and vandalism. Their motto was 'deeds not words'.

On 4th June 1913, the King's horse was running in the Epsom Derby. As it turned the corner for the home straight, a woman named Emily Davison ducked under the guard rail and ran onto the race course. The King's horse knocked Davison to the ground, and she died four days later in hospital. Nobody can be sure whether Davison intended to die in protest, or simply to interrupt the race. Either way, the Suffragists and Suffragettes would have to wait another five years before Parliament responded to their demands.

1914 | The First World War

When German forces marched through neutral Belgium and attacked France in the summer of 1914, Britain was compelled to defend her continental neighbours. Britain declared war on Germany on 4th August 1914. At first, British soldiers were promised a short and successful conflict – 'it will all be over by Christmas' being the cheerily optimistic verdict of troops leaving for France. In fact, the opposite was true. Having helped to check the German advance that autumn, British troops dug into trenches along what became known as 'the Western Front'. It was a stalemate, and here British troops would remain largely stationary for the rest of the war. Conditions in the muddy, rat-infested trenches were horrific.

The First World War was a war of attrition, with each side employing the latest military technologies to wear down the enemy – machine guns, tanks, airplanes, barbed wire, and poison gas. There was a widespread propaganda campaign encouraging young men to 'join up', and over two million volunteered to fight on the Western Front. However, this was still not enough. In January 1916 the government introduced conscription for the first time in Britain's history, compelling all men aged between eighteen and forty-one to fight.

1916 | The First Day of the Somme

By the summer of 1916, British military command had decided that an all-out offensive against the German line was needed to break the stalemate on the Western Front. Before the attack, the British artillery subjected the Germans to an eight-day-long bombardment, dropping 1.7 million shells on their trenches. British troops were led to believe that the German trenches would be so weakened by this bombardment, they would be able to walk calmly over no man's land unopposed.

In reality, the British bombardment had failed to break through the Germans' heavy concrete bunkers. On the morning of 1st July 1916, the British troops attacked, only to be met with a hail of machine gun fire from German trenches. Many men were sitting targets, having been caught in the German barbed wire. Nevertheless, wave after wave of British soldiers were sent over the top. By the end of the day, the British had suffered 58,000 casualties, with 19,000 dead. It was the most brutal day in the history of British warfare. The Battle of the Somme would ultimately bring an estimated 620,000 casualties to the French and British sides and up to 600,000 Germans. When the battle ended in November 1916, only 7 miles of land had been taken.

1918 | Armistice Day

In the Spring of 1918, the German army attempted a final offensive, but they so exhausted themselves in doing so that the allies were able to counter-attack. In a series of battles known as the 'Hundred Days', the armies of France, Britain and America (who had joined the war in 1917) pushed the Germans out of France. The German army surrendered, and on the eleventh hour of the eleventh day of the eleventh month 1918, armistice (peace) was declared. As in countries across Europe, a whole generation of young British men had been destroyed by war. Some 700,000 British soldiers had died, with another 1.7 million wounded, and many suffering from severe psychological trauma for the rest of their lives.

Parliament did find a way of rewarding the British people for their sacrifices. In February 1918, Parliament passed the Representation of the People Act, granting the vote to all men over 21 years of age. Women were granted the vote for the first time, but it was restricted to those over the age of 30 or who owned property. It would take another ten years before women were granted the right to vote on the same basis as men.

1922 | The BBC

In 1898, the Italian inventor Guglielmo Marconi opened Britain's first ever radio factory in Chelmsford, Essex. It produced 'wireless' radios – so called for their ability to transmit sound without wires. In 1922, a group of leading wireless manufacturers formed the British Broadcasting Company – a private broadcaster financed by the sale of wireless radios. Under Parliament's recommendation, the company was dissolved and reformed in 1927 as the British Broadcasting Corporation, or BBC. The BBC operated under a Royal Charter, which granted it a monopoly over British broadcasting financed by the payment of a 'licence fee' by wireless radio owners. BBC programmes were to have no advertisements, and be designed – in the words of its first Director-General Lord Reith – to 'inform, educate, and entertain'. This rather paternalistic, middle-class outlook earnt the BBC its nickname 'Auntie B'.

The BBC's monopoly on broadcasting spread to television, until the development of commercial television in the 1950s, and commercial radio in the 1970s. Since its inception, the BBC has had an unmatched impact on British broadcasting, developing comedies such as 'Monty Python' and 'Only Fools and Horses', dramas such as 'Doctor Who', children's programmes such as 'Blue Peter', and cookery shows such as the 'Great British Bake Off'.

1926 | General Strike

The soldiers who survived the First World War were promised a 'land fit for heroes' when they returned. However, the British economy no longer enjoyed its pre-eminent position in the world, and by 1925 it had gone into depression. British employers responded by extending working hours and cutting wages. In particular, a government commission proposed that mine-owners reduce miners' wages by 13 per cent, and increase their shifts from seven to eight hours. When the mining unions protested, the mine-owners responded with a lockout, denying employment to all union members.

The Trades Union Congress (TUC) asked members of unions across Britain to show solidarity with the miners and go on strike. On 4th May 1926, Britain found itself experiencing its first and only General Strike. Around 1.7 million people stayed off work, bringing industries such as printing, gas, electricity, and transport to a shuddering halt. Some feared that Britain was on the verge of revolution. The army were brought in to move vital supplies, and volunteers offered to drive buses. However, after nine days, the TUC called off the strike, without a single concession being made to Britain's miners. The General Strike had failed, and British workers were left feeling betrayed.

1936 | Abdication

By the end of his life, King George V was nervous about passing on the throne to his eldest son, Prince Edward. King George V believed the royal family should represent tradition and moral probity, but his good-looking and charming son loved all things modern: jazz, cocktails, nightclubs and aeroplanes. Prince Edward would even appear in public without a hat! King Edward VIII was crowned in January 1936. Later that year Edward's subjects learnt that their king was in a relationship with an American socialite called Wallis Simpson. Shockingly, Mrs Simpson had divorced one husband, and was in the process of divorcing a second.

Divorce was still looked upon with strong disapproval in English society, and it was simply unimaginable that Mrs Simpson could become Queen. The Prime Minster Stanley Baldwin told King Edward that he would have to choose between his throne or Mrs Simpson. So, in a live radio broadcast to the nation, King Edward told his subjects that he could no longer continue as King without the 'woman I love'. Edward VIII abdicated, passing the throne on to his younger brother King George VI. He lived out his retirement from royal duties with his wife in Paris.

1940 | Dunkirk

On 10th May 1940, Hitler launched his blistering invasion of France, and a small British army was stationed in Europe to withstand the attack. Three weeks later, the Germans had pushed over 300,000 British troops back to a long, windswept beach on the northernmost coast of France called Dunkirk. The British troops were trapped, with German planes flying overhead and the English Channel separating them from home. On 26th May Britain's new Prime Minister Winston Churchill ordered the Royal Navy to sail to Dunkirk and rescue the British troops, but its large destroyers were unable to reach the soldiers assembled on the shallow beach.

In response, Churchill launched Operation Dynamo. British citizens who owned small boats were asked to sail to Dunkirk, and relay soldiers from the beach to the destroyers. Around 800 fishing smacks, lifeboats, tugs and yachts answered the call, and Churchill's 'Armada of little Ships' set sail for France. The British Army were forced to abandon all of its tanks, vehicles and equipment, but the great majority of soldiers were safely brought home to England. The army had narrowly avoided total annihilation, but as Churchill reminded the House of Commons: 'Wars are not won by evacuations.'

BLACK-OUT 9.37 p.m. to 4.18 a.m.

Sun	rises	4.59 a.m.
	sets	9.7 p.m.
Moon	rises	3.37 a.m.
	sets	6.20 p.m.

DAILY SKETCH, MONDAY, JUNE 3, 1940.

BOMBS ON NORFOLK:
PAGE THREE

Daily Sketch

No. 9,695 (E**) MONDAY, JUNE 3, 1940 ONE PENNY

DUNKIRK DEFENCE DEFIES 300,000

FOUR-FIFTHS OF B.E.F. SAVED:
STORY ON PAGE THREE

'THE NAVY'S HERE'—WITH THE ARMY

" We have been able to embark and save more than four-fifths of the British Expeditionary Force, which the Germans claim to have encircled," said Mr. Anthony Eden, our War Minister, last night. Here is a crowded British port at which some of them arrived. Vessels of all kinds have come alongside. Every ship is packed with men. More pictures of the homecoming of British and French troops from Flanders are on pages 8 and 9.

BRITAIN'S LAST WORD TO ITALY:
BACK PAGE

1940 | The Battle of Britain

Following the evacuation of Dunkirk, Winston Churchill addressed the British people over the radio. He told them, 'the battle of France is over. I expect the battle of Britain is about to begin.' Churchill was correct, but before Hitler could safely send his troops over the English Channel, he had to wipe out the Royal Air Force (RAF). From August 1940, the German air force (known as the Luftwaffe) launched an all-out attack on British airfields and aircraft factories. In response, squadrons of British Spitfires and Hurricanes engaged the Luftwaffe in dogfights over the skies of Britain, often watched by citizens on the ground.

The RAF's fighter planes were able to outgun and outmanoeuvre the German bombers, whilst the German fighter plane – the Messerschmitt – was handicapped by its low fuel capacity. From mid-August to mid-September, the RAF lost 832 planes compared to the Luftwaffe's 1,268. On 17th September Hitler postponed his invasion, and the Battle of Britain was over. In a radio broadcast to the nation, Churchill paid tribute to the airmen who fought in the Battle of Britain, stating: 'Never in the field of human conflict, was so much owed, by so many, to so few.'

1941 | The Home Front

More than any war before or after, the Second World War required the total mobilisation of British society. Conscription was introduced for men aged eighteen to forty-one, and with so many men fighting abroad, women entered the workforce in their millions. In 1941, Parliament called upon all young, unmarried women to register for war work. Women took on jobs as mechanics, farmers, engineers, munitions workers, and bus drivers. Though women never served in combat, over 640,000 women joined the armed forces, carrying out roles such as delivering aircraft, driving ambulances and code-breaking.

From 1940–1, British cities suffered aerial attacks from the Luftwaffe in a period known as the Blitz, which killed around 40,000 civilians and destroyed large parts of urban Britain. To escape the Blitz, around 3.5 million people (mostly children) were evacuated to the countryside, or to British dominions such as Canada and Australia. Food shortages meant that rationing was introduced, ensuring all British civilians received the same quantity of basic foods such as milk, eggs and breakfast cereal. Britain's home front was under constant threat during the Second World War, but the war has also been remembered for the strong sense of unity felt by British society.

1945 | VE Day

On 8th May 1945, the Allies accepted the unconditional surrender of the German army, and Victory in Europe (or VE Day) was declared, prompting celebrations all over Britain. Bunting and Union flags lined the streets of towns and cities, where impromptu street parties and parades took place. Pubs were allowed to stay open late, and an all-night party was held in Piccadilly Circus, London. The Royal Family made eight public appearances on the balcony of Buckingham Palace, and later that night the future Queen Elizabeth and her sister Margaret secretly snuck out of the Palace to join the revellers in the streets.

Once the parties had died down, Britain was faced with the task of rebuilding herself. Half a million homes had been destroyed, and some 450,000 British soldiers and civilians had lost their lives, along with the same number of deaths from the British Empire and Commonwealth. The Prime Minister Winston Churchill was hailed as a national hero, but when he led the Conservative Party into the next General Election, the British people decided he was not the man to rebuild Britain. That job was given to Clement Attlee, whose Labour Party won a landslide election victory in July 1945.

1948 | The NHS

Labour swept to power in the 1945 General Election on the promise that they would build a welfare state for the British people. This plan was based on the 1942 Beveridge Report, in which the social reformer William Beveridge proposed the 'abolition of want' through state provision of housing, benefits, pensions and – most importantly – a National Health Service (NHS). This service would be free at the point of delivery for any British citizen, funded entirely by the taxpayer.

Until this point, Britain's health service was run by a patchwork of charities, local councils, and private institutions. Those who were too poor to afford health insurance either had to run up large debts paying for treatment or simply suffer their illness. In creating the NHS, the state would take control of 2,750 of Britain's hospitals, something that was widely opposed by Britain's doctors. The Health Minister Aneurin Bevan was tasked with winning Britain's doctors round, and did so by offering generous salaries for NHS employees. The National Health Service was finally created on 5th July 1948, launched by Anuerin Bevan at the Park Hospital in Manchester. Their first patient that day was the thirteen-year-old Sylvia Beckingham, admitted for treatment of a liver condition.

1948 | The *Empire Windrush*

In 1948, Parliament passed the British Nationality Act, which granted British citizenship to the inhabitants of Britain's overseas colonies. That same year, the HMT *Empire Windrush* set sail from Kingston, Jamaica, with 492 West Indian immigrants, seeking to start a new life in England. One such immigrant was Sam King, who like many on-board the ship had served in Britain's armed forces during the Second World War, as an aircraft fitter for the RAF. King went on to become mayor of Lewisham, the first black mayor of a London borough.

This first wave of Commonwealth immigrants became known as the 'Windrush Generation'. They heralded a new chapter of this country's history, transforming England into a multi-racial society. Over the next few decades, hundreds of thousands of immigrants arrived from across the former British Empire, from nations such as India, Bangladesh, Pakistan, the Caribbean, and Hong Kong. They played a vital role in addressing Britain's post-war labour shortages, taking jobs in transport, industry and retail. The Windrush Generation changed the face of British society. Today, there are over half a million people of Caribbean descent living in Britain, and around 14 per cent of Britain's population was born overseas.

EMPIRE WINDRUSH

LONDON

1953 | Coronation of Queen Elizabeth II

On 6th February 1952 King George VI died aged fifty-six. The next in line to the throne was his daughter Elizabeth, who at the time was on a royal tour to Kenya with her husband Phillip. That day Elizabeth returned to her Kenyan home after a night spent wildlife spotting, to find out she was now Queen of the United Kingdom and the Commonwealth Realms.

Elizabeth's coronation took place on 2nd June 1953 – the thirty-eighth monarch to be crowned in Westminster Abbey. An estimated three million people crowded onto the streets of London to watch their new monarch leave Buckingham Palace in her golden state coach. Elizabeth swore the coronation oath in front of 8,000 guests including the then Prime Minister Winston Churchill (who had won the General Election two years previously), stating: 'The things which I have here before promised, I will perform and keep. So help me God.' The BBC provided live coverage of the event, allowing millions more to watch the coronation around the world on television, made possible as this technology was more popular and affordable by this time. At the time of writing, Elizabeth II remains Queen at the age of 92, making her the longest reigning monarch in British and English history.

1956 | Suez Crisis

Opened in 1869, the Suez Canal is one of the most important manmade shipping routes in the world, linking the Mediterranean to the Red Sea through a 120-mile stretch of northern Egypt. From 1875, the canal was co-owned by Britain and France, and played a vital role in the British Empire's global trade.

In 1956, Egypt had a new nationalist President named Colonel Nasser. He seized the Suez Canal from Anglo-French ownership and announced the Canal to be under Egyptian state control. The British, French and Israeli Prime Minsters decided to take action in response: Israel attacked Egypt on their border, providing a pretext for a joint British and French force to invade Egypt and retake the canal. The Anglo-French intervention was a military success, but was condemned by the United States of America and the United Nations. Under pressure from the international community, Britain and France were forced to withdraw their troops from Egypt. The Suez Crisis left Britain and its leaders humiliated, and became symbolic of Britain's wider decline as an imperial force during the post-war era. Once a global superpower, Britain was now firmly in the shadow of its American cousins.

1966 | World Cup win

In 1966 the FIFA World Cup was held in England. The hosts were not favourites to win, especially after England opened the tournament with a dismal 0–0 draw against Uruguay. However, England went on to secure a place in the final at Wembley against West Germany. It proved to be an extraordinary match. England went 2–1 up in the 77th minute, but with just a minute left on the clock, Germany equalised, forcing the game into extra time. England manager Alf Ramsay told his players, 'you won it once, now go out and win it again!'

After 11 minutes of extra time, England striker Geoff Hurst was controversially awarded a goal by a Russian linesman. Then, with just 1 minute to go, the England captain Bobby Moore picked out Geoff Hurst unmarked in the German half. As Hurst raced towards the German goal, English fans began invading the pitch. The BBC commentator Kenneth Wolstenholme declared, '...some people are on the pitch, they think it's all over...', then Hurst sent the ball thundering into the German goal, and Wolstenholme concluded, '...it is now!' In front of 98,000 delirious fans, Bobby Moore shook hands with Queen Elizabeth II, and lifted the World Cup for the first and only time in English history.

In March 1963 the Beatles released their debut LP, *Please Please Me*. It was followed by a string of number-one singles: 'I want to Hold Your Hand', 'Can't Buy Me Love', and 'She Loves You' – then the biggest selling single in British history. The Beatles' manager Brian Epstein had achieved a stroke of commercial alchemy by dressing the excitement of American Rock and Roll in the guise of four 'cheeky chappies' – John, Paul, Ringo and George – from Liverpool. The Beatles started the year as relative unknowns used to slogging their way through the nightclubs of Liverpool and Hamburg, but finished the year a national sensation. Mobs of screaming teenage fans descended on every performance, as cameras captured scenes of uncontrollable hysteria. 'Beatlemania' had been born.

The following year, the Beatles broke America, with more than 70 million people watching their appearance on the *Ed Sullivan Show*. In 1966, John Lennon declared 'we're more popular than Jesus now'. The Beatles were emblems of the 'swinging sixties': four confident and attractive young men who symbolised the birth of a socially liberated age. Pop music, youth culture, and (according to the poet Philip Larkin's famous claim) sexual intercourse were all born in 1963.

1979 | Thatcher becomes Prime Minister

By the 1970s, Britain's economy was wracked by double-digit inflation, whilst union strikes brought industries and public services to a halt. Margaret Thatcher, the new Conservative Party leader, blamed Britain's difficulties on Labour government policies. She was elected as Britain's first female Prime Minister in May 1979. Thatcher immediately introduced laws to curb union power, privatise state industries, and allow council home tenants to buy their houses. Facing opposition from all corners, Thatcher showed her trademark determination at the 1980 Tory Party Conference. She told those asking her to perform a 'U-turn': 'I have only one thing to say. You turn if you want to... the lady's not for turning.'

Thatcher's privatisation of state industries hastened the decline of British manufacturing, giving way to today's service economy. Deregulation of the banking sector turned the City of London into a global financial centre. But these reforms came at a cost, with whole communities losing their livelihoods and unemployment rising above three million. Today, Thatcher remains a controversial figure, celebrated by some as the saviour of Britain's fortunes, and bemoaned by others as the harbinger of individualism and inequality. However, few can disagree that Thatcher's reforms transformed life in Britain.

1989 | Invention of the World Wide Web

Tim Berners-Lee, the son of two computer programmers, graduated from the University of Oxford in 1976 with a degree in physics. By 1989, he was working as a software engineer at CERN, the particle physics laboratory in Geneva, Switzerland. Scientists from all over the world wanted to access research produced at CERN, and Berners-Lee grew frustrated with how difficult it was for this information to be shared.

Berners-Lee was aware that computers could network with each other through a fast-developing technology called 'the internet'. In 1989, he proposed that the CERN laboratory should place their findings 'online' in a publically accessible format that scientists could retrieve from anywhere around the world. Over the next two years, Berners-Lee designed a web 'server' where information would be stored, and a web 'browser' where information would be displayed. In 1991, he launched the world's first website – http://info.cern.ch. Berners-Lee was aware of the world-changing potential of his invention, so he decided to allow anyone to access and display information on the World Wide Web for free. Today, the way people around the world share information has been completely transformed by Berners-Lee's invention. Remarkably, he has never made a penny from anyone wanting to use the internet.

1994 | Opening of the Channel Tunnel

The idea of building an undersea tunnel linking England with France was first proposed in 1802. The first actual attempt to build such a tunnel began in 1881, but the project was abandoned after a year due to fears that it would threaten Britain's national security. Over the following century, numerous proposals were put forward but none were successful, until a consortium of British and French companies were awarded the project in January 1986. Public opinion favoured a tunnel cars could drive through, but this aroused fears of ventilation issues and accidents. Instead, passengers could either travel by train, or drive their cars into specially designed train wagons.

The Channel Tunnel required digging a 31-mile undersea tunnel which was to link Folkestone in Kent, United Kingdom, with Coquelles, Pas-de-Calais, France. It took six years to complete and involved the work of 13,000 people. The Tunnel was opened in 1994 by The Queen and the then President of France, Francois Mitterrand.

In 2017, around 350 trains pass through the tunnels each day, carrying an average of 28,500 passengers, 7,000 cars, 140 coaches, and 61,500 tonnes of freight. There is little hiding who is visiting who on holiday: 85 per cent of car passengers travelling through the Tunnel are British!

1997 | Death of Princess Diana

Diana Spencer married Prince Charles on 29th July, 1981 at St Paul's Cathedral, London. At first they seemed to enjoy a fairy-tale marriage, and together they had two boys named William and Harry. But in reality, Charles and Diana's relationship was deeply unhappy. They separated in 1992, and Princess Diana devoted much of her life to humanitarian work, travelling the world to raise awareness of issues such as AIDS and landmines. Public interest in Diana was insatiable, and she became the most photographed woman in the world.

In 1996, Diana began a relationship with Dodi Fayed, and the tabloid press followed their every step. In the early hours of 31st August 1997, a car in which Dodi and Diana were travelling crashed into the wall of a tunnel in Paris. Dodi was killed instantly and Diana died later that morning, aged only thirty-six. Britain entered an intense period of national mourning. The Royal Family were roundly criticised for staying silent, but the newly elected Labour Prime Minister Tony Blair managed to capture the public feeling by stating Diana would forever be remembered as 'the people's princess'. The following month, thirty-two million people watched Diana's funeral on television, still the most viewed event in British history.

1997 | Harry Potter

In 1990 Joanne Rowling had the idea for a series of novels whilst sitting on a delayed train from Manchester to London King's Cross. The novels would follow an orphan named Harry Potter who on his eleventh birthday is invited to attend Hogwarts School of Witchcraft and Wizardry. Rowling immediately began sketching out the plan for a seven-book series, detailing Potter's struggles with a Dark Wizard named Lord Voldemort.

Living as a single mum in Edinburgh and working as a teacher, Rowling completed her first novel *Harry Potter and the Philosopher's Stone* in 1995. It was rejected by twelve different publishers, until Bloomsbury finally published a print run of just 500 copies under the name J.K. Rowling in 1997. The *Philosophers' Stone* quickly became a word-of-mouth hit and over the next two years sold 300,000 copies. Rowling published six sequels, culminating with *Harry Potter and the Deathly Hallows* in 2007 – the fastest selling book in history. Rowling's books have broken almost every record conceivable, selling over 500 million copies and being translated into seventy languages, inspiring countless children to start reading. The spin-off Harry Potter films have grossed more than $7 billion, making Rowling the world's first (and still only) billionaire author.

2012 | London Olympics

For three weeks during the summer of 2012, London enjoyed a warm glow of contentment as the Olympic Games returned to the capital for the third time in the Games' history. Many doubted London's ability to pull off such a complex infrastructure project, with recent debacles such as the Millennium Dome and the rebuilding of Wembley Stadium fresh in the public's memory. But it proved to be a triumph, thanks in no small part to an army of 70,000 unpaid volunteers, known as the 'Games Makers', who were given responsibility for day-to-day running of the events.

Film director Danny Boyle created the opening ceremony, which evoked both Britain's history and its contemporary culture. Highlights included Mr Bean playing the keyboard part to the theme music of the film *Chariots of Fire*, and James Bond (supposedly) parachuting out of a helicopter and into the Olympic Park with the Queen. By the end of the games, Great Britain were placed third in the medal tally, with a remarkable individual performance from Mo Farah who won two Olympic Gold medals. But the undisputed star of the games was the Jamaican Usain Bolt, who became the first sprinter to win the 100m and 200m races in two consecutive Olympic games.

2016 | Brexit

Ever since Britain joined the European Economic Community (later to become the European Union) in 1973, Britain's Conservative Party has been split between its pro- and anti-EU factions. In the run up to the 2015 election, the Conservative Party Prime Minster David Cameron knew that one of the greatest threats to his electoral fortunes came from the anti-EU United Kingdom Independence Party (UKIP) taking votes from the Conservatives. So, Cameron promised that if the Conservatives were to win the general election, they would hold a national referendum on whether Britain should remain a member of the EU.

Cameron's Conservatives won the 2015 election, and set the EU referendum date as Thursday, 23rd June 2016. On the day of the vote, there was a significant national turnout of 72 per cent. To the surprise (and horror) of much of the media and political classes, the 'Leave' side won by a narrow margin of 4 per cent. An intense period of political turmoil followed, with a Conservative leadership campaign and General Election both held within a year of the result. At the time of writing, Britain is set to leave the European Union on 29th March, 2019. But there remains a mountain of bureaucratic detail to be resolved before that can go ahead.